LITTLE
PRAYERS
&
FINITE
EXPERIENCE

RELIGIOUS PERSPECTIVES
Planned and Edited by

RUTH NANDA ANSHEN

RELIGIOUS PERSPECTIVES • VOLUME TWENTY-FOUR

LITTLE
PRAYERS
&
FINITE
EXPERIENCE

by *Paul Goodman*

HARPER & ROW, PUBLISHERS

NEW YORK, EVANSTON, SAN FRANCISCO, LONDON

The Little Prayers by Paul Goodman that are listed below originally appeared in
the following publications:

Nos. 1–8
The Lordly Hudson (New York: The Macmillan Company). Copyright © 1962 by
Paul Goodman.

No. 9
The Empire City (Indianapolis: Bobbs-Merrill Co., Inc.). Copyright © 1959 by
Paul Goodman.

Nos. 10–36
The Lordly Hudson (New York: The Macmillan Company). Copyright © 1962 by
Paul Goodman.

Nos. 37–60
Hawkweed (New York: Random House, Inc.). Copyright © 1967 by Paul Goodman.

Nos. 61–72
North Percy (Los Angeles: Black Sparrow Press). Copyright © 1968 by Paul
Goodman.

Nos. 73–86
Homespun of Oatmeal Gray (New York: Random House, Inc.). Copyright © 1969,
1970, by Paul Goodman.

Nos. 87–110 appear in this book for the first time.

FIRST EDITION

STANDARD BOOK NUMBER: 06–063325–5

LIBRARY OF CONGRESS CATALOG CARD NUMBER: 72–78070

RELIGIOUS PERSPECTIVES

VOLUMES ALREADY PUBLISHED

• v •

CONTENTS

RELIGIOUS PERSPECTIVES:

Its Meaning and Purpose by RUTH NANDA ANSHEN ix

RELIGIOUS PERSPECTIVES

Its Meaning and Purpose

RELIGIOUS PERSPECTIVES represents a quest for the rediscovery of man. It constitutes an effort to define man's search for the essence of being in order that he may have a knowledge of goals. It is an endeavor to show that there is no possibility of achieving an understanding of man's total nature on the basis of phenomena known by the analytical method alone. It hopes to point to the false antinomy between revelation and reason, faith and knowledge, grace and nature, courage and anxiety. Mathematics, physics, philosophy, biology, and religion, in spite of their almost complete independence, have begun to sense their interrelatedness and to become aware of that mode of cognition which teaches that "the light is not without but within me, and I myself am the light."

My Introduction to this Series is not of course to be construed as a prefatory essay for each individual book. These few pages simply attempt to set forth the general aim and purpose of the Series as a whole. They try to point to the principle of permanence within change and to define the essential nature of man as presented by those scholars who have been invited to participate in this intellectual and spiritual movement.

Modern man is threatened by a world created by himself. He is faced with the conversion of mind to naturalism, a dogmatic secularism and an opposition to a belief in the transcendent. He begins to see, however, that the universe is given not as one existing and one perceived but as the unity of subject and object; that the barrier between them cannot be said to have been dissolved as the result of recent experience in the physical sciences, since this barrier has never existed. Confronted with the question of meaning, he is summoned to rediscover and scrutinize the immutable and the permanent which constitute the dynamic, unifying aspect of life as well as the principle of differentiation; to reconcile identity and diversity, immutability and unrest. He begins to recognize that just as every person descends by his particular path, so he is able to ascend, and this ascent aims at a return to the source of creation, an inward home from which he has become stranged.

It is the hope of RELIGIOUS PERSPECTIVES that the rediscovery of man will point the way to the rediscovery of God. To this end a rediscovery of first principles should constitute part of the quest. These principles, not to be superseded by new discoveries, are not those of historical worlds that come to be and perish. They are to be sought in the heart and spirit of man, and no interpretation of a merely historical or scientific universe can guide the search. RELIGIOUS PERSPECTIVES attempts not only to ask dispassionately what the nature of God is, but also to restore to human life at least the hypothesis of God and the symbols that relate to him. It endeavors to show that man is faced with the metaphysical question of the truth of religion while he encounters the empirical question of its effects on the life of humanity and its meaning for society. Religion is here distinguished from theology and its doctrinal forms and is intended to denote the feelings, aspirations, and acts of men, as they relate to total reality. For we are all in search of reality, of a reality which is there whether we know it or not; and the search is of our own making but reality is not.

RELIGIOUS PERSPECTIVES is nourished by the spiritual and intellectual energy of world thought, by those religious and ethical leaders who are not merely spectators but scholars deeply involved in the critical problems common to all religions. These thinkers recognize that human morality and human ideals thrive only when set in the context of a transcendent attitude toward religion, and that by pointing to the ground of identity and the common nature of being in the religious experience of man the essential nature of religion may be defined. Thus, they are committed to reevaluate the meaning of everlastingness, an experience which has been lost and which is the content of that *visio Dei* constituting the structure of all religions. It is the many absorbed everlastingly into the ultimate unity, a unity subsuming what Whitehead calls the fluency of God and the everlastingness of passing experience.

The false dichotomies, created by man, especially by Western man, do not exist in nature. Antinomies are unknown in the realm of nature. The new topology of the earth implies the link between an act and a whole series of consequences; and a consciousness of the individual that every time a decision is made it has distant consequences which become more precisely determined.

Furthermore, man has a desire for "elsewhere," a third dimension which cannot be found on earth and yet which must be experienced on earth: prediction: detailed statement referring to something that is to happen in the future; projection: combining a number of trends; prevision: that which is scientifically probable and likely to happen; prospective: the relation between present activity and the image of the future; plan: the sum of total decisions for coordinated activites with a goal, both spiritual and material, in mind.

The authors in RELIGIOUS PERSPECTIVES attempt to show that to *be* is more important than to have, since *being* leads to transcendence and joy, while having alone leads to apathy and despair.

Man has now reached the point of controlling those forces both outside himself and within himself which throughout history hemmed in decision-making. And what is decisive is that his new trend is irreversible. We have eaten of this new tree of knowledge and what fifty years ago seemed *fate* has now become the subject of our deliberate choices. Therefore, for man, both in the East and in the West, the two basic questions are: What proper use can we make of our knowledge both for the spirit and for the body and what are the criteria for our choices. To the correct answers to these questions which conform to the new reality can the continuity of human life be preserved and the human person related not only to the present but also to the past and therefore to the future in a meaningful existence. The choice is ours.

These volumes seek to show that the unity of which we speak consists in a certitude emanating from the nature of man who seeks God and the nature of God who seeks man. Such certitude bathes in an intuitive act of cognition, participating in the divine essence and is related to the natural spirituality of intelligence. This is not by any means to say that there is an equivalence of all faiths in the traditional religions of human history. It is, however, to emphasize the distinction between the spiritual and the temporal which all religions acknowledge. For duration of thought is composed of instants superior to time, and is an intuition of the permanence of existence and its metahistorical reality. In fact, the symbol[1] itself found on cover and jacket of each volume of RELIGIOUS PERSPECTIVES is the visible sign or representation of the essence, immediacy, and timelessness of religious experience; the one immutable center, which may be analogically related to being in pure act, moving with centrifugal and ecumenical necessity outward into the manifold modes, yet simultaneously, with dynamic centripetal power and with full intentional energy, returning to the source. Through the very diversity of its authors, the Series shows that the basic and poignant concern of every faith is to point to, and overcome the crisis in our apocalyptic epoch—the crisis of man's separation from man and of man's separation from God—the failure of love. The authors endeavor, moreover, to illustrate the truth that the human heart is able, and even yearns, to go to the very lengths of

[1]From the original design by Leo Katz.

God; that the darkness and cold, the frozen spiritual misery of recent times are breaking, cracking, and beginning to move, yielding to efforts to overcome spiritual muteness and moral paralysis. In this way, it is hoped, the immediacy of pain and sorrow, the primacy of tragedy and suffering in human life, may be transmuted into a spiritual and moral triumph. For the uniqueness of man lies in his capacity for self-transcendence.

RELIGIOUS PERSPECTIVES is therefore an effort to explore the *meaning* of God, an exploration which constitutes an aspect of man's intrinsic nature, part of his ontological substance. This Series grows out of an abiding concern that in spite of the release of man's creative energy which science has in part accomplished, this very science has overturned the essential order of nature. Shrewd as man's calculations have become concerning his means, his choice of ends which was formerly correlated with belief in God, with absolute criteria of conduct, has become witless. God is not to be treated as an exception to metaphysical principles, invoked to prevent their collapse. He is rather their chief exemplification, the source of all potentiality. The personal reality of freedom and providence, of will and conscience, may demonstrate that "he who knows" commands a depth of consciousness inaccessible to the profane man, and is capable of that transfiguration which prevents the twisting of all good to ignominy. This religious content of experience is not within the province of science to bestow; it corrects the error of treating the scientific account as if it were itself metaphysical or religious; it challenges the tendency to make a religion of science—or a science of religion—a dogmatic act which destroys the moral dynamic of man. Indeed, many men of science are confronted with unexpected implications of their own thought and are beginning to accept, for instance, the trans-spatial and trans-temporal dimension in the nature of reality.

RELIGIOUS PERSPECTIVES attempts to show the fallacy of the apparent irrelevance of God in history. This Series submits that no convincing image of man can arise, in spite of the many ways in which human thought has tried to reach it, without a philosophy of human nature and human freedom which does not exclude God. This image of *Homo cum Deo* implies the highest conceivable freedom, the freedom to step into the very fabric of the universe, a new formula for man's collaboration with the creative process and the only one which is able to protect man from the terror of existence. This image implies further that the mind and conscience are capable of making genuine discriminations and thereby may reconcile the serious tensions between the secular and religious, the profane and sacred. The idea of the sacred lies in what it *is*, timeless existence. By emphasizing timeless existence against rationalism as a reality, we are liberated, in our communion with the eternal, from the otherwise unbreakable rule of "before and after." Then we are able to admit that all forms, all symbols in religions, by their negation of error and their affirmation of the actuality of truth, make it possible to experience that *knowing* which is above knowledge, and that dynamic passage of the universe to unending unity.

God is here interpreted not as a heteronomous being issuing commandments but as the *Tatt-Twam-Asi:* "Do unto others as you would have others do unto you. For I am the Lord." This does not mean a commandment from on high but rather a self-realization through "the other"; since the isolated individual is unthinkable and meaningless. Man becomes man by recognizing his true nature as a creature capable of will and decision. For then the divine and the sacred become manifest. And though he believes in choices, he is no Utopian expecting the "coming of the Kingdom." Man, individually and collectively, is losing the chains which have bound him to the inexorable demands of nature. The constraints are diminishing and an infinity of choices becomes available to him. Thus man himself, from the sources of his ontological being, at last must decide what is the *bonum et malum.* And though the anonymous forces which in the past have set the constraints do indeed threaten him with total anarchy and with perhaps a worse tyranny than he experienced in past history, he nevertheless begins to see that preceding the moral issue is the cognitive problem: the perception of those conditions for life which permit mankind to fulfill itself and to accept the truth that beyond scientific, discursive knowledge is nondiscursive, intuitive awareness. And, I suggest, this is not to secularize God but rather to gather him into the heart of the nature of matter and indeed of life itself.

The volumes in this Series seek to challenge the crisis which separates, to make reasonable a religion that binds, and to present the numinous reality within the experience of man. Insofar as the Series succeeds in this quest, it will direct mankind toward a reality that is eternal and away from a preoccupation with that which is illusory and ephemeral.

As I have said above, we are in the presence of a serious crisis of knowledge. The crisis could be defined as the end of social determinism or the end of social fatalism. In other words, our era, for the last two generations, represents a fundamental break with all past history. For we now possess a rapidly growing ability to control the forces which throughout history hemmed in individual decision-making and, even more important, which made the collective social processes appear as inexorable events ruled by pseudo-natural laws.

Up to the middle of the nineteenth century, for example, the population trend was ruled by nothing but biological laws, and the balance of population was regulated by 'natural' events such as Malthus' three horsemen: war, hunger, pestilence. Now a change has been brought about not only by individual control of birth-rates and death-rates, but also by collective application of public health policies and findings of epidemiology. Other examples of equal significance could be mentioned.

Here, however, I wish to refer to a trend which takes us back to the Renaissance. During the last two generations we have made a quantum jump, or in Hegelian terms, the quantitative changes have altered the quality of our life world. And what is decisive is that this trend of which I speak is *irreversible*. We have eaten of this new tree of knowledge, and what fifty years ago appeared to be *fate* has now become the subject of our deliberate choices.

Thus, I must repeat, if choices are to be made, the first question is: on what foundations of knowledge? And the second question is: what are the criteria for our choices? Therefore, it is the hope of *RELIGIOUS PERSPECTIVES* to try to point to at least some of them, for our dilemma is one of criteria for our judgments.

For man is now confronted with his burden and his greatness: "He calleth to me, Watchman, what of the night? Watchman, what of the night?"[2] Perhaps the anguish in the human soul may be assuaged by the answer, by the *assimilation* of the person in God: "The morning cometh, and also the night: if ye will inquire, inquire ye: return, come."[3]

RUTH NANDA ANSHEN

[2]Isaiah 21:11.
[3]Isaiah 21:12

PREFACE

ASKED FOR a book on religion, I have only the following little prayers written during thirty-five years. They are rather my religious facts than my ideas; they are what I *did* (or how I escaped) in certain crises, composing poems rather than behaving some other way. I am a writer, and to write it, to say it, is very much how I cope.

But are they prayers? The words "God," "Creator Spirit," "Father," and so forth, that occur in these particular statements, are words that I otherwise never use in either practical actions or in thinking my own thoughts. In psychotherapy, which is the nearest I know to formal religious exercises, I do not use this vocabulary. The poems are prayers, but the prayers are just poems; the religious words are "poetic license." I doubt that I meant them to assert anything as propositions, nor to be earnest requests. They do not say anything, I hope.

Yet there they are. Pretty soon I imitated myself in writing them, and after a while I collected them.

I started writing these stanzas in imitation of the chorales of J. S. Bach. The very first (here no. 27)—written in Chicago in 1937 —is direct from "Ruht wohl dein heilige Gebeine" in *The Passion According to St. John.* I wanted something to express a resting place in a larger sacred story I was writing, and that I tore up. (I—with most of us—do not have sacred stories that we believe in.) I kept the poem. But I do not have any congregation to join in chorales. So my hymns soon became resting places only for myself, saying at certain moments just how it was, however it was.

To avoid the heavy tread and clank of Protestant hymns when they do not have good music, I chose to rime in glancing assonances, to overflow the couplets and stanzas, to vary the tetrameters with shorter or longer verses—to tailor the verses to the motion of my thought, since the poems were personal not public statements. Yet I am bemused at myself how I have rigorously stuck to the form—the latest little poems were written a week ago. (It took me twenty-five years to allow myself, sometimes, a third or fourth stanza.) Evidently, when I undertake to cope with the despair, horror, joy, or confusion of my existence by writing how it is, I am bound to do so in eight four-beat lines rimed *a-a*, *b-b*, *c-c*, and *d-d*. Whatever charming traits art may have, it is obsessional; and a writer soon becomes his own classical model. Yet it has been good, in straits, to have *any* convention that works for me, when little else does.

The order of the collection is factitious. I would have liked to put the poems in exact chronological order of writing, but it is irretrievable. This is how I arranged them for publication in various volumes of poetry, with a few written later. I notice that every few years the style is dryer; and "thou" tends to become "you."

The essay *Finite Experience* was notes for a course at the University of Hawaii, in 1971. Students often asked me how I *am*—how I go about it. Because of the well-known alienating conditions of modern times, they are baffled how anybody can do anything, and I—in their eyes—have "made it." So I thought I would once try to spell it out in detail.

But naturally my answer had to be in terms of my own conditions, for instance as an aging bisexual in bad health, with a literary gift; and therefore it was pretty irrelevant to them where they were, vigorous, sexually more practical, at a loss for vocation. And naturally, I end up with the same Little Prayers, since they say how it has been. The essay is a commentary on the poems.

Come to think of it. Since

> homespun of oatmeal gray
> without a blazon is the flag
> that I hold up and do not wag

—why would anybody salute?

Yet such an essay is not useless. If I can show how my way of being roughly adds up, it is likely—and encouraging—that other ways also add up. And for me it has been interesting to find, not that my ideas and attitudes and behavior are consistent—I have always felt consistent *enough*—but that this can be written down and shown.

Waimanalo, Hawaii
April 1972

LITTLE

PRAYERS

&

FINITE

EXPERIENCE

I
LITTLE PRAYERS

(from *The Lordly Hudson*)

1. Creator Spirit, who dost lightly hover
    whence I know not, and why to me I never
        questioned, come. Do visit thy lover
        after Thy long absence. I turn over

    awaking in the morning: Thou art not
    there to my touch nor is a substitute
        there, but nothing nothing at all to talk
        to and make love when I awake.

2. O spirit wise, somewhere shine!
    so I can squander me again.
        I ask it, if ever I tried hard
        to eke me out a livelihood

    from my grudging city, and if ever
    I have been patient to preserve
        opportunity my sweet
        muse, my darling, my flirt.

II

FINITE EXPERIENCE

1. Within My Horizon

1. I CAN'T think abstractly. Like everybody, I suppose—how would I know?—I start from concrete experience, but I have to stick to it. "Force" or "cause" always finally means to me that I give a push, or make it out of wood like a carpenter. Failing this, I cultivate my acre like a dumb peasant, and it grows maybe in spite of my efforts. I feel with Faraday when he said, "I never could know a fact that I didn't see"—he didn't mean that he was empirical, for all science is empirical, but that, the son of a blacksmith, he had to devise apparatus and produce the fact. As a writer, I almost never have a further purpose than just saying it; the structure that I find or put in the words is *universale in re*.

In these notes, paying attention to what I do, "bracketing it off" as Husserl says, I am spelling out where this leads me and how it traps me. It is both happy and unhappy.

I am faintly disgusted by ideas, *universale ante rem*. I had a Platonic spell as an adolescent, and my guess is that it is masturbating with an image that is distasteful, rather than just with my body. Or ideas are a surfeit, I can't keep them down.

I get lost, quickly confused, when people reason from classes of things, *universale post rem*. I usually dislike what they come out with because it is frigid and irrelevant. When I do admire abstract formal thinking, like mathematics, I take it like music, concrete after all. But then I am baffled how it can apply to anything beyond itself, as it seems to.

• 3 •

3. The tons of trucks that thunder by
perturb not me who thread my way.
    The sun is roaring through the smoke
    by grace on me who stand and look.

   I do not know if happiness
   will show before me like a face
       or rise within me like a song,
       deliberately I move along.

4. The flashing shadow of the sun
in the bloody window made me turn
    and face his face, and I saw
    over his shoulder You.

   Everywhere I look about
   are there outlines of truth and art
       breeding in the dark of this
       moment at the edge of the abyss.

2. Let me give an example. In Western calisthenics we characteristically aim at an abstract standard of health and performance and devise exercises toward it; for the vital functions, we do chest-expansion and tone the heart, and we do push-ups and pull-ups for strength. In Prussian military exercises the goal is further predetermined, to create a martial attitude, pelvis retracted, chest up, chin in.

Chinese *tai-chi,* so far as I understand it, tries to activate every possible muscle by the flowing passage from posture to posture. So it is less predetermined by an abstract standard or extrinsic goal; it is tailored to the natural species. But it not tailored to me, where and how I am.

The right exercises use the available powers that I have—limited by my tensions, inhibitions, illness, inattentiveness, disuse—and try to develop them, by the smallest increment possible, to what I don't do but could do. As the case is with me, the best next motion is often to relax. The art of the trainer is to notice what my body "wants" to do, and to suggest the appropriate posture and movement. The theory is that my organism tends to actualize itself if I stand out of the way. It is an article of faith.

The appropriate motion may be passionate: shouting at someone, weeping, or recoiling in fear. It may be intellectual: brow becoming perplexed; loosening watchful teeth, eyes, and breathing and becoming confused; or saying a complete sentence how I am. It may be "physical": throwing a punch or hauling water.

There are no right exercises without an object in the environment, though I may not yet know what it is.

3. Environment is not the roundabout space but the place *of.* It is the eco-niche in which only one species lives and reproduces, though it seems to be crowded with too many other species. The *amate* tree that I used to lie under in Cuernavaca was a whole aviary of ethnic neighborhoods at different levels and shadows. Conversely, there are big areas that are empty and undeveloped, but I doubt that they are underdeveloped.

5. Novices of art
    understate
        what has them by the throat
        the climax; You speak out

    for me, spirit who affright
    me in the lonely night,
        nor do I know till I express it
        the message boiling in my breast.

The Empire City

6. Thee God we praise for this complete
    book that overwork and doubt
        and pain could mar but not prevent
        because Thy spirit still was sent.

    Such as it is, this now belongs
    also among the created things
        whilst I relapse, Thy dying fact
        more spent, more sullen, and more racked.

It is the place of me now. It is not the climate that counts, nor even the day's weather; but that it was hot in the field leeward of the hill, to be playing a competitive game in which my relations with the others were too thick. I ought to have worn a hat. I did not chew my breakfast because of my bad teeth, and anyway my diet was deficient in vitamin E.—After I had the heart attack, the doctor forbade me to go swimming in the river, saying, "Of course, it's the ideal exercise for your condition, but there might always be a sudden emergency. Also, no driving for two months." Wise advice: be prudent. Quite impossible to follow, for it is the essence of the sudden that it happens all of a sudden, imprudently. Trying to avoid the sudden I can work myself into a state all of a sudden.

Goethe's contrary advice was probably wiser: "We commit some folly just to live on a little." But which? when? He—evidently!—knew the answer—as it turned out. The proof of a sage is that he lasts.

4. Experience is prior to the "organism" and the "environment," which are abstractions from experience. It is prior to "I" and "that there," which are abstractions. They are plausible, perhaps inevitable abstractions, except for moments of deep absorption. They are said by every natural language, and it is the devil to try to invent a phenomenological language that avoids them. But we must be careful not to forget the matrix from which they are abstracted. There is no function of an organism that does not essentially involve its environment—we breathe air and walk by gravity and ground. No feeling that does not address the environment—anger that there is an obstacle to reaching, or an insult to organic integrity; grief that there is a hole in the environment, or a loss there that must be mourned through. If emotions did not signal something about the environment, they would not have been inherited and have survived; they tell the relation of organism and environment, and they spur us to cope.

Conversely, the actual environment, the place, is what is se-

7. Guarantor of the harvest, who
   to Noah pledged if he would sow
      and delve some good would come of it
      and sent him Rainbow your spirit

   —though not yet have you promised me
   that the laborer will enjoy—
      I offer you this play
      wistfully waiting for my pay.

8. In how few hours I
   have put myself awry
      and live again in fear
      till I escape from here.

   Askew and queer is my
   existence in the only
      world I make, impatient,
      arrogant, ignorant.

lected, structured, and appropriated by the organism.

Aristotle put it well: When sensory power is actualized, when there *is* experience, the sense organ is the *same as* the sensed object. "The object of sight is the oval of vision."

Experience is neither "subjective" nor "objective." Its proper nouns are Here, Now, Next, Thou, We, rather than I, It, Past, Future. It is impossible to talk such a language, but it is the genius of literature to recapture primary experience by combining narrator and narrative in ongoing plot. A man of letters will at any moment become personal in his essay; a sociologist may not.

Ideally, the operational style in science should recapture primary experience, but it invariably lacks courage and does not really bring in the investigator as an animal and person; instead, his operations themselves are described as objects. On the other hand, those who write the sociology or psychology of science usually, though not invariably, avoid the adventure and the objective discoveries in the field, the things that make it worthwhile to talk about scientists altogether. Instead, they become politically polemical or they psychoanalyze, introducing further abstractions. It is not interesting that Newton was mad unless we show how the inverse-square law of gravity is mad—which it perhaps is; and to the extent that the law of gravity was not altogether mad, we should revise our notions of what a madman is—we certainly should.

5. In my experience, experience occurs in finite but good-sized chunks. Each chunk roughly hangs together internally, but I have never experienced that All is One or that everything is connected. I have also never had a conversion or "blinding flash of insight," but very frequent insights, connections new to me, that I greet with a beck of the head saying "Hm," but rarely "Aha!" or "Wow!" When I have an insight, the rough structure is sharper or more vivid, rarely new.

The structure of experience is clearer if I pay attention without staring. If I can scan and meditate. I don't know—I have never

9. Father, guide and lead me stray
   for I stumble forward straight my way
      undeviating, I do not
      notice the pleasant bypaths that

   make us this world surprising nor
   the precipice that sinks before.
      O give me ground for next a step
      to stagger walking in my sleep.

10. By trials too hard for me beset
    with awkward courage toward my death
       I stagger; every usual
       task I perform and, as I fail,

    fashion the art-works to me given;
    but lust is mercifully riven
       from me with hope, for ever our
       task is measured to our power.

really tried it—if there is a method, like the scientific method, that works to produce insight. Many of the fruits attributed to method are just a style of reporting what was already seen without the method. I myself usually pay attention after I have had an insight rather than to produce one, for it is easier to attend to what is interesting, what is becoming interesting.

Except when I am in pain or ill, my chunks of experience are quite sizable and complex, not small details or poor. There is plenty of room in them for me. (But because of chronic ailments I have suffered a lot of pain, and then my experience is constricted and boring.) I have never felt the wish to expand my consciousness, whether by drugs or political movements, or by identifying with the new generation—I just envy their vigor and sex. Indeed, I have found it hard to cope with the amount of consciousness I have.

My finite sizable chunks of experience are probably the same as the "normal" response to Rorschach cards: rarely seeing a Whole, rarely restricted to Small Details. In fact, however, my own Rorschach readings are inauthentic; I either see the cards too esthetically, as patches of shade and color and white space, or I see them too matter-of-factly as reproductions of ink-blots. So in the theater I notice made-up actors, painted scenery, and artful speeches; I do not experience a theatrical illusion. I am sure I am missing something, but thereby, in my opinion, I better do get to know the playwright or whoever has been managing these things.

6. "Surrounding" finite experience must be what is not experienced. (This is an article of faith.) What, if anything, can be said about it from what is actual in experience?

In awareness there is a boundary of which one is still dimly aware, Husserl's "horizon"; and let us consider this in two different ways. First, if I turn to *it,* then what is beyond the boundary enters awareness. Whichever way I move, comes into being new space. To attend to the boundary is a standard device of psycho-

11. Help, Angel Courage! for I wooed
    confusion and willingly betrayed
    my blind intelligence in ord-
    er to visit with the Lord,

    but now in the too early dusk
    I panicky have gotten lost
    and cannot make it. Give O ang-
    el Courage me thy hand.

12. O God of fire and the secret mus-
    cles of the world, restore my lust
    and happy power as I used,
    for somewhere now I have got lost

    and am confused and impotent,
    yes, gazing with bewilderment
    in such a face as how Thy dea-
    rest angel looks, looks up at me.

therapy: if there is an absence of feeling, trace the boundary of what *is* felt, e.g. the air in the nostrils; then how far can you feel beyond the previous boundary, e.g. air in the sinuses. Awareness itself seems to generate energy. They tell me there is a neuro-physiological basis for this effect.

But the contrary tack is even more remarkable. If I withdraw further from the boundary by concentrating on the center, then the emptier the backgound is, the brighter and more structured the figure in the foreground. I take it that this is the idea of Yoga concentration. For my own theoretical purposes, I feign the hypothesis that energy flows from the emptying background and vivifies the figure in the foreground. I rely, by an act of faith, precisely on what I do not experience. Tao says, "Stand out of the Way." The implication is that there is then *new* energy, and theoretically, I like to deny the conservation of energy. But perhaps it is energy that we have dammed up and now set free, the tack that Horatio takes in *The Empire City*: "Let go, and it will move."

If in either case, attending to the boundary or withdrawing from it, the void is fertile, then it is very well that experience is finite.

Assume, as Berkeley pointed out about the oval of vision, that in general the field of experience is constant in size. Then, as we exclude what we do not intend to notice, the object of notice looms larger, nearer. It would take us over, except that I become dizzy. When I recover, I have lost the object and am having a different experience of constant size. This is Yang and Yin. Like the spaceman in *The Empire City*, I fail to experience the moment when *that* world which I am approaching becomes *this* world into which I have fallen.

7. I like a scientific explanation that is solidly grounded in what we do not know, for instance *The Origin of Species*. Darwin starts with varieties, from which he builds everything, and he knows nothing at all about the nature of variation. He did not know

13. Heavy silence, Lord, dim eyes,
     dull ears, and dubious a guess,
        I offer Thee as that which is.
        My tithe is this blind daze

     as I to work return
     without reward for past work done
        and for the work I do begin
        without desire or hope. Amen.

14. Like Adam firmly walking to
     the farm-work that he knew to do
        in deep confusion, for the grim
        news of everyday to him

     happened each thing by surprise
     like a fist between the eyes
        —so let me day to day work on
        in this thick cloud that has sunk down.

Mendel's laws of inheritance, nor chromosomes and genes, nor the causes of mutation. What is astounding is that he knew he did not know, instead of inventing some nonsense. But it is as if his ignorance let him really scrutinize the varieties, in domestication, in geographical distribution, in geological sequence. They were the matter, the material cause, dark but potential for *his* investigation. So Harvey had no way of connecting arteries and veins, but the blood circulated anyway.

There is an essential ignorance that clouds experience and prevents a good figure from forming in it; this gives me a headache until I find the missing clue; for instance, if the plot of a story doesn't work itself out because I have neglected something in the characters. But there is an essential ignorance in which I float happily, and that even seems to brighten what I do know, by contrast.

Put it the opposite way. To explain something in experience, we may pursue a chain of causes exploring back and back into what we do not know. But then the cause we arrive at will be abstract, and reduce the present concrete experience to what follows from other investigations, prior causes. It does not explain enough in the present experience. I prefer an explanation that saves the present experience as it is and copes with the problems that *it* poses, and tells me what it's made of, how it happens, how it works, how it hangs together, how to make it, where it's tending. Such explanations are themselves likely to raise questions and ask for other explanations, but then that will be a different concrete experience.

8. Pursuing a chain of causes, we may find necessary causes. But sufficient causes must be found in the concrete present.

To explain the negative, a failure, an illness, the lack of a necessary cause, we can draw on an abstraction. Kurt Goldstein used to point out that an injury to the optic nerve might prevent seeing; but one does not see with the optic nerve, nor with the eye, but with the whole organism, when there is light, etc. So

15.   On the highroad to death
        trudging, not eager to get
          to that city, yet the way is
          still too long for my patience

      —teach me a travel song,
      Master, to march along
          as we boys used to shout
          when I was a young scout.

16.   Blessed is the landscape that around
        the turning will come at a joyous bound
          into view! for God who holds my hand
          is a wise explorer as our way we wend.

      And He explains to me in simple English
      the geology and botany that flash
          on my new soul, and cities in turmoil
          where He points out what is still practical.

Hughlings Jackson: "One cannot explain a positive effect [an actual symptom] by a negative cause." By psychoanalysis of a childhood fixation, Freud explained why Leonardo did not paint more; he did not pretend to explain why he painted. The medievals said, *Natura sanat non medicus:* a physician may remove a source of infection or supplement a vitamin deficiency, but it is not he who restores function.

Unlike mathematicians, scientists may not reason by listing the possibilities and eliminating all but one. For the unknown may contain another possibility of explanation. It is likely to, or somebody would have reasoned it out long ago. Science must start from a fact. Aristotle: "Dialecticians reason from concepts; a scientist syllogizes from real premises."

9. Besides a rough structure, an intrinsic meaning, finite experience is usually ongoing and has a direction, an intrinsic end-in-view. So it has value. It wants to realize itself, practically or theoretically.

Since primary experience is prior to the distinction between subjective and objective, it is not yet a question whether the value is in the object or is felt into it by me. I myself do not remember any "value-free" experiences—perhaps one does not notice such. When an experience is consummatory, has no tendency either to fulfill itself or to try not to be, it is all the more value-laden, beautiful or tranquil, dismaying or despairing: "Stay!" or "I wish I were dead." For philosophers like Aristotle or Spinoza, the value of an achieved truth was happiness itself, the mind in action, or *hilaritas*, God's joy.

It is discouraging that recently scientists want to say that science is value-neutral, while indeed they are practicing beautiful personal and social virtues: honesty, accuracy, adventurousness, perseverance, humility, statement in due form, concern for public replication. Their science is rich with these virtues as well as truth, elegance, and possible utility. It must be that they have lost their heroic *élan* and are on the defensive. I think they are

17. Your kingdom is within me sure
    but I do not inhabit there
        with You and me. But searching for
        myself among the strange and poor

    and violent I go because
    my gentle gifts I despise.
        And yet one day I shall be known
        for a native son.

18. At last I know—for friends have said—
    my shameless public ways have made
        me scorned and fail and lonely in
        this teeming city. Lord, between

    us, I would not do otherwise
    for Thy name's sake among these
        Babylonians, although I long
        for the people of whom I am one.

frightened by the inevitable abuse of the forces they unleash, so they hasten to disown responsibility, rather than trying politically to prevent the abuse, which is all any of us can do. (I do not think a scientist, or anybody else, has the option *not* to do his thing.)

The nature of things is wonderfully amenable to the heroic virtues of science. One can easily conceive a universe that does not reward patient effort, or where no setup is publicly replicable; but as Einstein put it, "God is subtile but not mean"—He does not deceive, the evidence is not planted to mislead us. God is hard to scrutinize but (to Einstein) He is not inscrutable. William Bateson used to urge his students to "cherish your exceptions," just as the Good Shepherd leaves the flock to rescue the lamb who has gone astray.

To bypass the problems of psychophysical interactions, Russell postulated that they happened in a "neutral stuff"; but this formulation comes to the same thing as saying "incarnate spirit," and it is as ideological. It is interesting that Russell used such self-denying language about reality when elsewhere he speaks so passionately about the erotic drive of his active intellect; it is as if he will never get what he loves because she's a cold fish. His friend Whitehead more complacently saw Deity emerging from matter like Aphrodite from the foam.

The naturalist school of novelists have also cultivated the notion that the facts are value-neutral, but by their treatment they disown the facts and are transparently saying, "Damn them." These same value-neutral facts happen to build into the writer's *summum bonum*, developing and climactic plot, tragedy.

Among academics, insistence on the value-neutral feels like chronic low-grade spite. It used to be the custom, from Aristotle until quite recent times, to introduce a course of lectures with a panegyric on the subject, its utility, or how ennobling to study it just for itself. Nowadays, in my observation, professors seem resentfully to disown what they are teaching. Indeed, among the younger radical sociologists of knowledge, the disposition is to show that a disinterested scholar, who values just what he is

19. Jail and blows, being a coward,
     I dread, but I am inured
        to be misunderstood,
           because the common reason, God,

        communes with me. Let them refute
     the propositions I have put
        with nail and hammer on the door
           where people pass, upon the square.

20. My friends are ruined, I am in dismay,
     the blow will reach also to me;
        fearful, desperate, and resourceless
        we are, and heavy is our loss

     already. Heaven help us therefore
     because our strength and prudence are
        unable to the traps and foes
           that men have strewn, and we arouse.

doing, is a witting or unwitting agent of the Central Intellignece Agency. At least this is not value-neutral.

To sum up, I stick pretty close to the concrete and finite, that comes in sizable chunks with a rough structure and an ongoing tendency and is immersed in ignorance, a void that is sometines fertile. Such experience is roomy enough for me, usually meaningful, and sometimes valuable. And I have priggishly been pointing out its advantages.

10. Put in a different light, I am stuck with a poor way of being and thinking. Since I can't, or won't, readily think abstractly or symbolically, I can't get out of the stream when it would be useful to do so. Let me try to say it accurately. I am not drowning; I am not like an aphasic who cannot conceptualize his experience and so is vulnerable to "catastrophic reactions" (Kurt Goldstein); I conceptualize very well. I am only occasionally swamped and burst into tears. But I do not have moments of free choice. I probably do not know what freedom feels like. I will soon discuss my anarchism—I do not ground it in freedom. (Is it unconsciously a lust for freedom from my own tyranny, my *will* to be concrete and finite and make sense?)

My choices have been unusually autonomous, originating from myself, but—as I compare myself to some people—*I* never made them, and I never *made* them. I did not choose to be a writer, to live with my wives, to teach in schools, to be a Dutch uncle to the young, etc. Rather, I drifted into these because they were what I could do with my available means and opportunities, or was asked to do in actual situations when there seemed to me to be no other alternatives, or they were where my desires landed me though it was not what I wanted. These landing places then worked out and persisted because I could farm them well, and they chose me. I don't complain that I have been forced into anything. On the contrary, I am canny and stubborn, except for a short spell, in resisting and rejecting what doesn't suit, what doesn't have some kind of sense, what violates my honor and integrity. I can resist what is incompatible with my concrete expe-

21. "Child, resent it not; by grave
      offenses you yourself have
          armed against you every creature." No,
          Father; if today I throw

      beaten my armor down,
      it is to go lighter. Sound Thy dawn
          bugle and collect us bright
          hundreds who are few but right.

22. My anger has become
      a settled rage. I am calm
          but I no longer wish to touch
          human flesh with tender lust.

      Lord, give me back my lust to touch
      human flesh, or else teach
          me some otherwise to make sense
          of my experience.

rience, but I have no perspective to choose something else.

Goethe's advice to the youth was good, "Do what you can, not what you want," for the youth was alienated, a product of *Sturm und Drang*, and needed a material connection with the world. It is not good advice for me.

My inability to stand outside the stream of the concrete, watch it, and freely choose, is especially disastrous when I am bogged down in compulsive repetitions that don't work. Surely it would often be better for me to make an abstract judgment of what I want and where I am, to will a clear-cut decision, and to use purely instrumental means to succeed. Rather than to persist like Oblomov in Goncharov's book.

But for some reason I feel it is wicked to use a calculated means to get what I want, for instance to end up in bed with some one, though I do *not* disapprove what I want. I will not use such means, and I do not get what I want.

I do not disapprove my vices, but I disapprove a calculated plan to succeed in satisfying them. As I will say it later, happiness must happen, be a proof that we live in paradise, or why bother?

Yet the concrete is at least real, even if really lousy. The abstract wish is usually delusory, and the calculated means don't work anyway. Goethe again, "Beware what you wish for in your youth, for you will end up getting it in your middle age."

A married couple torment each other; if they break up, they will probably be happier, and surely be healthier, at least for a time. Yet they might not then have any one important in their lives, and is empty happiness worth it? The decision to break up is probably correct only if they are in fact involved elsewhere. Like science, personal relations must start from facts, not possibilities.

11. Since they are not organized by abstract concepts, my finite chunks of experience often do not add up; but I regard this rather complacently. I am usually consistent enough without having to be systematic. My Father's house has many mansions, and personally I am not very ambitious; I work hard to improve each

23.   Now dare I anything, O Warden
of the drunk and careless, guard me!
for the reins that stay my course
and hinder me are loose;

as forth I go, and forth I shall,
my blond and black horses gallop
toward a wreck that I forecast
with little interest.

24.   Creator of the worlds, O joy
of speed! and when the powers that lie
latent into being break
I shall confront the onward wreck

because I am in love with
the nature of things unto death
and as they loom, say, "Lo!"
Lord rescue me, this road I go.

shining hour, but I don't much care if I get anywhere. I don't hanker after any overwhelming climax of experience, a surpassing orgasm, or an expansion of consciousness.

But it is another matter when various chunks of experience do jar badly or are in outright conflict; or when drifting on one, I find myself on the shoals for the next. Each chunk of life has its intrinsic and therefore justified value, but I have no standard to make them commensurate, and little system to organize them practically. I am not referring especially to basic "tragic" conflicts, between absolute values like compassion and truth, honor and loyalty, love and duty, in which I am sometimes trapped like any other serious person; but just the embarrassments that afflict a man who is busy, desirous, and disorganized. Suddenly I must cope with too many commitments, interests that are contradictory.

My pathetic expedient is to affirm both sides of the contradiction and carry on, not even hoping that something will turn up to extricate me, but just because I am at a loss what else to do, and I proceed by routine. In serious tragic conflicts, such a loyalty to contradictory absolute values is *chosen* and it has grandeur; it deserves the *deus ex machina* who saves the hero in some Greek plays; and maybe it is better to die than to betray an absolute though finite good. But in ordinary hang-ups like mine, I anxiously act out each side more strenuously than is necessary; I get no satisfaction on either side; there is not enough time for anything and there is still more miscalculation; friction increases. Till finally I am so weary that I have to withdraw from the field and lose both parties, and I have a host of psychosomatic symptoms to preoccupy me instead.

They say that it feels good to stop beating your head against a wall, but a person like that immediately develops other aches and pains.

12. But it's not so bad as that; I am omitting one factor, art, that is always either present in my experience or very near. It has

25. When hope and hate are so
    much mixed, how shall I know?
       shall I rage or shall I rest?
       —Thou therefore urge upon what is best,

    I will perform it, for Thy word misleads
    all my researches savage into reasons
       ever springing alive, and Thy voice
       in my amazement is still peace.

26. Upon his loyal son
    my father did look down
       and made him brave a few days
       to say the truth he knows.

    Now thou Creator Spirit
    him do not desert
       when he announces news
       he does not know he knows.

made the difference, I think, between my life being wretched or just unhappy.

In a novel *Making Do* I draw the older man, one of the two protagonists, quite literally from myself, except that I explicitly will not let him be an artist in his distress and fortitude; he can't have this out. I do have it.

Though I cannot will much for myself, I have a strong will to shape. If something goes well, I finish off by praising it. If it goes badly, I make something of it anyway by saying it. And the *products* of art add up; they join thousands of years of human culture around the world, bringing me into a great company. What could have been a fragmented existence has become a regular and respected career. (To be sure, if I hadn't had the disposition of an artist, I would have had some other disposition.)

—I am driving to the University around Koko the old volcano, to give a lecture that is not useful, nor do I much care if the students learn anything. I don't believe in modern universities. I am here to spend the winter in Hawaii and I have to have some occupation and excuse for being here. There are so many young fellows at the University, maybe I can find a lover for my loneliness. Suddenly, arching the highway is a great Hawaiian rainbow, the "gentle shock of mild surprise" that unlooses a poem. One foot of the rainbow is planted in Manoa Valley on the campus. And the point of the poem is that I will not find a pot of gold there, nor will I bring one. It turns out to be a good little poem. —I certainly do not have experiences in order to write poems about them. But what I experience is certainly congenial to the poems that I will write.

It is a hard question if art-will is *my* will. The urgency to write a poem rather comes to me; I cannot neglect it without bad consequences, boredom, distraction, insomnia. The subject, the "first line," usually chooses itself and often says itself; it is what I have noticed in a peculiar way, not my way—Wordsworth analyzes it well. The arc of the whole, as a beginning, middle, and end, is not planned, though I steer it and as a critic after the fact

27.   Rest well thy weary head and heart
      and work no more, my sorely hurt;
         thee God when in the pit of night
         thy sight is sealed can new create.

      Each breath, I know, is almost more,
      poor child of lust, than life can bear
         and forethought has betrayed thy foot.
         Let help come if it will or not.

28.   Manlike my God I make, nor fear
      to be an idol's fool, for
         so hard I think of man the thought
         crumbles into absolute

      un-Nature. Oh, and He will save
      me in the little work and love
         I lust in day by day until
         my name He elects to call.

I can demonstrate it if anybody wants to know. The product, and having produced it, does nothing for me in the way of making me happier or wiser—it is a typical repetitive act springing, as Freud said, instead of a symptom. (Of course a symptom is itself an artistic act.) Admiring readers have not gone out of their way to give me what I need.

In other senses, it is my poem. I am absorbed and happy while making it, that is, I do not notice how I am. I ride with its process. It is in my style and domesticates experience for me. It forms my further style, so that finally I experience what I can write. (I have learned to write in a style that allows me to experience a good deal.) I am proud of the product and I want fame for it and me.

13. For both better and worse, my writing is colored with the bias of the rest of my experience, toward the concrete, intrinsic, literal, and finite. Allegory makes me squeamish. The use of "symbols" seems to me to be sophomoric. Poetry with a moral or political purpose sets my teeth on edge. "Poetry" itself must not be an abstraction, a genre. The basis of poetic diction is good colloquial speech, and I do not intone my poems but read them for their prose sense. What moves me most is just saying the sentences and paragraphs, the motion and progress of meanings. The big pattern of motion—long and short passages, slow and quick passages—is the chief organization of many of my stories. The propositional truth of the sentences, their correspondence to reality, is indifferent to me, though I prefer not to be trivial or stupid. The possible effect on the readers never crosses my mind. (I do not care about them and they, catching the signal, give nothing to me while I age and die.)

The term "abstract art" has unfortunately gotten to be applied to precisely the most intrinsic and concrete art, the acting of the artist in the medium. "Abstract art" was so called because it dispensed with an external model; but when I here say that I do not "abstract," "abstraction" means generalization or class

29.   Saved! as I have faith
      and probable proof.
         But O God, am I weary
         of living in purgatory,

      in pain and fire tedious
      waiting for the voice
         of love that summons
         and the voice that responds.

30.   My world, my only! as I see
      soberly the necessity
         that so I fail, and my hurts
         are measured to my just deserts:

      fine! as every truth is fine.
      But that I change I do not find
         nor that I triumph by embrac-
         ing my fate, nor that I suffer less.

name, or external standard (including fidelity to a model), as opposed to intrinsic end-in-view. Words are about situations, but men of letters act literarily, concretely, they *tell* the situations.

Preparing a play, if an actress bogs down on certain lines, I strike them. I compose a speech that she can say well. I write in a new part for an actor because he looks like that. There are special architectural features to the stage—it is a church—so I remake the climactic scene in order to use them. It is better that the play has ringing voices and a grip on material reality than to try to say what I used to intend. Somebody can play the flute; why not a song for the flute, that beautiful instrument? Aristotle said, "Only the flute has the song of the flute," meaning that the matter, wood, is intrinsic to its form, the melody. Oddly, we still put our silver flutes among the woodwinds.

And it has its bad side. Since I stick so closely to concrete experience, I cannot really write fiction. I am uneasy if I replace the name of my lover in a poem by a made-up metrical equivalent, and art is hurt by fetishism. I can fantasize only my own dreams; in 1950 I dreamed of flying, so in *The Dead of Spring* they fly. I cannot act a character on the stage, I turn into wood without a melody. Even in delivering a lecture, I either just carry on a conversation with members of the audience, or I just think aloud for the audience, for I can be myself without embarrassment. The only psychoanalytic paper on writing that I ever wrote is on this theme: the inability to imagine fictions, sticking too closely to the actuality. I interpreted it to mean that there is something in the actuality that is repressed and *not* said, that pins the imagination.

I will try to make a balance. My literalness is a clog to flights of imagination, but it saves me from frigid fancies. It keeps me from standing apart and getting a view of what is, but by nagging just how it is I often find meanings that I didn't know I knew. And I do well what I do.

31.   Lord Nemesis and Reviver, who
         bless the past with its curse—I do
            therefore cling like death
            to what I might forget,

         may now this newborn that
         I rescued (although late
            and gracelessly) at least
            not torment me from the past.

32.   As blasted by a frost in May
         the lofty butternut to me
            no countryman looked dead, and shall
            I chop it down? I thought. But while

         I thought of it, sprouted a leaf
         and now my whole tree is rife
            with singing green, though I shall bear
            —forgive me, Lord—no fruit this year.

—I have among the Americans
    the gift of earnest speech
    that says how a thing is.
    If I do not, who will do it?

—Austere is the praise
        that I have learned to sing
    in verses out of my life
        as burgeons the spring.

33. Patience! for my only one
     my world is turning like the sun
         toward me her condescending face.
         And now behold! there is a race

     between the runners, long-awaited
     Fame and Death, which I am fated
         to watch with fascination deep
         as toward the finish-line they leap.

34. Lord, at the moment still and beating
     like the mighty heart of the great city
         asleep at dawn—when he and I
         standing outside our frantic folly

     aware of each other clung together,
     I thanked Thee! And now another
         time in memory
         and poetry I thank Thee!

2. Politics Within Limits

14. There is an odd abstraction "Society," thas has exercised a superstitious compulsion on political scientists since the time of Bentham, Comte, Hegel, and Marx; instead of the loose matrix of face-to-face communities, private fantasies, and shifting subsocieties in which most people mostly live their lives. It is understandable that fatherly czars or divine-right monarchs would have the delusion that all the sparrows are constantly under their tutelage as Society; and that Manchester economists would sternly rule out of existence all family, local, and non-cash transactions that cannot be summed up on the Stock Exchange. The usual strategy of Enlightenment philosophers, however, was to cut such big fictions down to size and to have simple real abuses to reform. But after the French Revolution, it was as if, to substitute for the slogan L'Ancien Régime, it was necessary to have a concept equally grand, Society.

Comte and Bentham wanted to make the big fiction of Society for real—Comte knew that it started as a fiction—in order to use it to tidy up "everything" or at least "the greatest good for the greatest number." For metaphysical reasons, Hegel was satisfied that the more socialized a man, and the more self-conscious of it, the more real he was. But the pathetic case is Marx, who concentrated on Society and indeed wanted to empower Society, presicely to get rid of it and go back to simpler personal and community existence.

35. God of the Fullness who in hours
     hast after my starving years
        filled my bowl and with garlands
        laden my outstretched hands,

     teach me again what it is
     I want, that I by long disuse
        and disappointment did forget,
        and now my brain is slow with surfeit.

36. All men are mad some way: O Lord
     Thou takest it not hard
        but when the rage is in me most
        by healing death deliverest.

     I shall not fear, my strongest will
     cannot deliver me to hell
        forever, for an Angel with
        a lamp appears in my death.

Certainly there are occasions when my existence as a mere member of Society is overwhelmingly important and not at all an abstraction, for example when they herd me onto a big airliner, with its backup of thousands of anonymous operatives and their schedules and instruments. But even so, after the initial shock, I soon recover and become restive for a more attractive seat-mate, or look for a couple of empties so I can stretch out and go to sleep, or I press my nose to the window and watch the clouds and the receding earth.

Usually my need for Society is satisfied by a very loose criterion: "Lucky is the man who can band together with enough of those like-minded with himself—it needs only a couple of hundred—to reassure him that he is sane, even though eight million others are quite batty." (*Empire City*, 1, 19, i)

By a good intuition, the best of the young dissidents disown abstract Society and want to be "just human." But they still reify it too much as the hostile "System," which exists but less than they think. Since they do not know concretely enough what they mean by "just human," they need a tangible adversary to give themselves shape. (But how, at my age, would I know what they mean?)

15. Most words of ordinary speech, of course, are simple abstractions, for classes of persons, things, relations, etc. Except in poetry and sociable chatter, the feel of the usual words is not Here, Now, Next—these are reduced to adverbs. Instrumental speech is likely to be abstract.

Simple abstractions need not be problematic. I can say, "There are our friends coming" and soon the words are "You—Here—Now—We—Next." But when there are difficulties—for instance, what if they are not our friends, and do not even speak our language and do not want to share our experience?—then we must resort to psychotherapy, politics, and pastoral theology to unmake alienation.

The critical question for me is how to have, or make, those

(from *Hawkweed*)

37. God, do you make me happier,
     for by my doing I am here
     and the outlook is even worse
     as I grow old. I have been cautious

     not prudent, and unusually thoughtful
     not wise. But indefatigable
     has been my love whether I could
     or not, which you count highly, God.

38. Dull, miserable, and ailing
     my way of life to which I clung
     stubbornly and often I
     disapproving proved my way

     cannot work, it is not viable,
     I am foredoomed to terrible
     years I cannot remedy.
     Life-saver, rescue me.

abstractions "Organism," "Environment," "History," so that they can possibly interact to reconstitute primary experience. I have written ten books on this question in various contexts. "To have an environment and not take it as an object, is Tao," said Chuang-tze. Sometimes I state my program in the form, "How to take on Culture without losing Nature," but that is already too abstract.

A conclusion I have reached is this: Like Luther, but unlike Hegel or Marx, I think that the way to overcome alienation is to go home and not on a tour through history and the realms of being. It is also true, however, that a man who is on the Way deviates and does not err.

16. In *Gestalt Therapy*, I reason my way into the subject as follows: If we envisage an animal moving, continually seeing new scenes and meeting new problems to cope with, it will continually have to make a creative adjustment. Selecting, initiating, shaping, in order to appropriate the novelty of the environment to itself, and to screen out what would destroy homeostasis. Adjusting, because the organism's every living power is actualized only in its environment. And the environment, for its part, must be amenable to appropriation and selection; it must be plastic to be changed and meaningful to be known. The precipice that you fall off is not your environment.

Aristotle says it succinctly, "Food is the unlike that can become like." Or, in a passage I have already quoted, "Perceiving is the identity of the object of sense and the activated sensory organ." —I like to quote Aristotle on these matters because he was the sophisticated climax of *prima facie* observations, and his formulations are drily pithy lecture notes. But I do not think his doctrine was different from Kant's, who was critical of two thousand years of philosophizing and came to the same *prima facie* observations, "The percept is blind, the concept is empty," "the synthetic unity of apperception," "judgment is not a categorial proposition."

Then I conclude, abnormal psychology is the therapy of dis-

39. I never did, Lord, believe
     that me you have preserved alive
     for any remarkable day
     or use—much as my country

     needs brains and bravery.
     But to be staring stupidly!
     to be drifting toward disgrace!
     to call for help too spiritless!

40. Stop keeping the home-things alive,
     my balky body, their grudging love,
     so forth: let them die if they want.
     I grew this avocado plant

     that never throve and survives skinny
     —it has ceased to be a symbol for me,
     let it dry! And yet I pour
     for pity's sake a glass of water.

turbances of creative adjustment, e.g. rigid or archaic responses.

And we can speak similarly of abnormal sociology: it is politics, to remedy institutions that hinder experience from occurring, e.g. roles rather than vocations, individuals or collectives rather than people in communities, whatever prevents citizens from initiating and deciding, or makes it complicated for craftsmen and professionals to practice.

There is no politics but remedial politics; often the first remedy is to take "Society" less seriously, and to notice what society one has.

17. As I review my books of social criticism and my occasional trips in therapy and politics, I am pleased at how they flow temperamentally from my biases about experience. My kind of anarchism, pacifism, and decentralism; opposition to mandarinism and schooling; emphasis on vocation and profession; ecology and neighborhood in physical planning; rural reconstruction; intermediate technology for underdeveloped regions; my "neolithic conservatism"—these are congenial to a bias for the concrete, finite, and artistic, *universale in re* and intrinsic end-in-view. Such as they are, my political ideas are authentic. —In fact, I haven't changed them since I was a boy, though there has been a lot of history since then. This must be partly because I don't learn anything, but it is partly because political truth is so simple that a boy can see it with a frank look, namely: Society with a big S can do very little for people except to be tolerable, so they can go on about the more important business of life.

It's an impressive list of topics that I spread myself thin over. To me, naturally, my opinions confirm one another by being coherent with one another wherever I look. The proof of a literary style is that it is viable over a wide range of experience, to say it.

A generalist is a man who knows something about many special sciences, in order to coordinate their conclusions in a system that has little relation to reality. A man of letters knows only a little

41. Whether I am close to death
or not, God of Breath,
    I do not know, nor what,
    dark God, to do with that.

    But my palms are wet and cold
    and a pure fear has taken hold
       of my heart. This I know,
       O simple God and true.

42. Lost—God help me—in a waste
where the dusk has fallen fast
    I cannot breathe and my cowardice
    is what it always was.

    No light, no guide, but now thank God
    my wet tears are welling hot
       and I can breathe in the black night
       and look about as I wait.

about some major human concerns, but insists on relating what he does know to his concrete experience. So he explores reality. A generalist is interdisciplinary. A man of letters finds that the nature of things is not easily divided into disciplines.

18. My social ideas are temperamentally mine, but they do not derive logically from my biases, as a doctrine. I would abhor a politics, pedagogy, or town-planning deduced from metaphysics or epistemology, or even scientifically deduced, rather than being pragmatic and not immoral. One must not manipulate real people because of an idea or a confirmed hypothesis. Indeed, I say "not immoral" rather than "moral" because positive morality, when used as a principle for action, can be more abstract and imperial than anything. There are far too many missionaries among my friends.

But instead of being abstract or moral, my corresponding defect is that I am an artist and fundamentally unpolitical. I don't (timidly) bestir myself to oppose anything or try to change it unless I first have imagined a simpler and more artistic way to do it, neater, making use of available materials, less senseless, less wasteful. If a bad situation is not amenable to my flash of inventiveness, I find it hard to identify with it as mine; I feel there's nothing that I can contribute. Meantime people are suffering. But a political person ploughs into the situation and makes a difference in it just by his action. Sometimes a good idea then turns up.

Artistic visions have their virtues. (Let me speak no evil of the creator spirit.) They are better than carping criticism. They give people a ray of light instead of the gloom of metaphysical necessity. Activism and ideology both do more harm than good. But art has the unpolitical self-sufficiency of art. I am not zealous to make my models real. And they have the timidity of being personal; I draw no strength from my fellows; I cannot lead and find it hard to follow.

One cannot rely on artists for a political message. Tolstoy

43. Fear with me walks abroad and where
     I live I am afraid. I am aware
     of many real dangers. Others
     are imaginary fears.

     Yet I seek neither, Lord, your peace
     nor the momentary happiness
     that I used to seek to ward
     off terror, Lord.

44. I have thought of my aunt singing
     when I was a child the air of Puccini,
     she is long dead who vividly
     returns to me in a memory

     and I, O God, shall be dead
     like her: is it this certitude
     that has destroyed my hope and joy
     and when I see beautiful things I cry?

makes war seem sublime and attractive. Homer makes it senseless and horrible.

19. But I mustn't overstate my diffidence. I, like anybody else, see outrages that take me by the throat, and no question of not identifying with them as mine. Insults to the beauty of the world that keep me indignant. Lies, triviality, and vulgarity that suddenly make me sick. The powers-that-be do not know what it is to be magnanimous; often they are simply officious and spiteful. As Malatesta used to say, you try to live better and they intervene, and then *you* are to blame for the fight that happens. Worst of all, it is clear from their earth-destroying actions that these people are demented, sacrilegious, and will bring down doom on themselves and those associated with them; so sometimes I am superstitiously afraid to belong to the same tribe and walk the same ground as they.

Yet men have a right to be crazy, stupid, or arrogant. It is our specialty. Our mistake is to arm anybody with collective power. Anarchy is the only safe polity.

It is a moral disaster to suppress indignation, nausea, and scorn; it is a political (and soon moral) disaster to make them into a program. Their right political use is negative, to band together to stop something.

It is a common misconception that anarchists hold that "human nature is good" and therefore men can rule themselves. But we tend rather to be pessimistic. We are phlegmatic because we do not have ideas. And men in power are especially liable to be stupid because they are out of touch with concrete finite experience and instead keep interfering with other people's initiative, so they make them stupid too. Imagine being deified like Mao-tse-tung or Kim Il Sung, what that must do to a man's character. Or habitually thinking the unthinkable, like our Pentagon.

20. Most anarchist philosophers start from a lust for freedom. Sometimes this is a metaphysico-moral imperative, with mission-

45.　The flashing summer we forecast,
　　　the bright beach, the dark forest,
　　　　and to tour the famous sights
　　　　of Europe, prospects of delight

　　　　—but Lord, our name is Joyless, we have
　　　dry voices and our looks are heavy.
　　　　Rescue us, we are immersed
　　　　in the sin of waste, which is the worst.

46.　By murder and arrest
　　　my frantic night is tossed,
　　　　awaking I look forward
　　　　either to peace, Lord,

　　　　or doom, in doubt which,
　　　bound home from far. And such
　　　　is my travel prayer
　　　　to the Savior.

ary zeal attached, but mostly it is a deep animal cry or religious yearning, like the hymn of the prisoners in *Fidelio*. They have seen or suffered too much restraint—serfdom, factory slavery, deprived of liberties, colonized by an imperialist, befuddled by the church.

My experience, however, has by and large been roomy enough. "They" have not managed to constrict it too much, though I have suffered a few of the usual baits, many of the punishments, and very many of the threats. I do not need to shake off restraint in order to be myself. My usual gripe has been not that I am imprisoned, but that I am in exile or was born on the wrong planet. My real trouble is that the world is impractical for me; by impatience and cowardice I make it even less practical than it could be.

For me, the chief principle of anarchism is not freedom but autonomy, the ability to initiate a task and do it one's own way. Without orders from authorities who do not know the actual problem and the available means. External direction may sometimes be inevitable, as in emergencies, but it is at a cost to vitality. Behavior is more graceful, forceful, and discriminating without the intervention of the state, wardens, corporation executives, central planners, and university presidents. These tend to create a chronic emergency that makes them necessary. In most cases, the use of power to do a job is inefficient in the fairly short run. Extrinsic power inhibits intrinsic function. "Soul is self-moving," says Aristotle.

The weakness of "my" anarchism is that the lust for freedom is a powerful motive for political change, whereas autonomy is not. Autonomous people protect themselves stubbornly but by less strenuous means, including plenty of passive resistance.

The pathos of oppressed people, however, is that, if they break free, they don't know what to do. Not having been autonomous, they don't know what it's like, and before they learn, they have new managers who are not in a hurry to abdicate. The oppressed hope for too much from New Society, instead of being vigilant to live their lives. They had to rely on one another in the battle,

47.   As if my purpose was to drown
       the shining ship I did abandon
          that was not sinking, rapidly
          she stood away, I did not try

       to swim, yet was about to cry
       help when I awoke and thereby
          helped myself, though I was wistful
          of the depths of the whirlpool.

48.   Surceaser of foreboding! I gave up
       myself to You to shatter and reshape
          in the plastic order of Your world,
          stranger than the world controlled

       by my rage. And You have bade
       me lay my plans in solitude
          with what initiative I can
          muster when my heart is broken.

but their solidarity becomes an abstraction and to deviate is called counterrevolutionary.

The possibility of my weaker position is that autonomous people might see that the present situation is disastrous for them, and that their autonomy is whittled away. They cannot help but see it. There is not enough useful work and it is hard to do it honestly or to practice a profession nobly. Arts and sciences are corrupted. Modest enterprise must be blown out of all proportion to survive. The young cannot find their vocations. Talent is stifled by credentials. Taxes are squandered on war, schoolteachers, and overhead. Etc., etc. The remedies for all this might be piecemeal and undramatic, but they must be fundamental, for many of the institutions cannot be recast and the system itself is impossible. A good deal could be made tolerable by wiping a good deal off the slate.

The aim of politics is to increase autonomy, and so it is mostly undoing. I like the Marxist formula "the withering away of the State," but it is the method, not the result.

21. The central organization of administration, production, and distribution is sometimes unavoidable, but it mathematically guarantees stupidity. Information reported from the field must be abstracted, and it loses content at every level; by the time it reaches headquarters it may say nothing relevant. Or it may say what (it is guessed) headquarters wants to hear. To have something to report, the facts of the field are molded into standard form and are no longer plastic. Those in headquarters cannot use their wits becasue they are not in touch. Those in the field lose their wits because they have to speak a foreign tongue, and can't initiate anything anyway. On the basis of the misinformation it receives, headquarters decides, and a directive is sent down that may fit nobody in particular. At each level it is enforced on those below in order to satisfy those above, rather than to do the work. When it is applied in the field, it may be quite irrelevant, or it may destroy the village in order to save it.

49. God, I prayed, to me restore
     some kind of thing to hope for
        that, only, creates energy
        from nothing for another day,

        but You instead have sent Your angel
     Indignation with his bugle
        to waken the Americans at midnight.
        Give me health and I will fight.

50. Not on our knees do we
     ask but hear our plea,
        Author of liberty.
        America our country

        has been leased out. We must and will
     reclaim her at our own peril,
        but do You faithfully ignite
        on the hilltop freedom's light.

The criteria for the success of such operations are abstractions like Gross National Product, Standard of Living, body count, passenger-miles, Ph.D.'s awarded. These at best have no relation to the common wealth, satisfaction of life, peace, experience of travel, or knowing anything. But at worst they impede the common wealth, peace, experience of travel, etc.

Nevertheless, central organization, that mathematically guarantees stupidity, is sometimes unavoidable; and just by existing, it exerts disproportionate power. This is a puzzler. The Articles of Confederation and the acrimoniously debated Federalist Constitution gave an answer that worked pretty well, in quite simple conditions, for almost thirty years.

22. I suppose the most sickening aspect of modern highly organized societies is the prisons and insane asylums, vast enclaves of the indigestible, that the rest live vaguely aware of, with low-grade anxiety.

We have been getting rid of the stupid but at least human notions of punishment, revenge, "paying the debt," and so forth. But instead, there persists and grows the Godlike assumption of "correcting" and "rehabilitating" the deviant. There is no evidence that we know how; and in both prisons and asylums it comes to the same thing, trying to beat people into shape, treating the inmates like inferior animals, and finally just keeping the whole mess out of sight.

The only rational motive for confining any one is to protect ourselves from injury that is likely to be repeated. In insane asylums, more than 90 percent are harmless and need not be confined. And in prisons, what is the point of confining those—I don't know what percent, but it must be fairly large—who have committed one-time crimes, e.g. most manslaughters and passional or family crimes, while they pay up or atone? People ought indeed to atone for the harm they have done, to get over their guilt and be "rehabilitated," but this is much more likely to occur by trying to accept them back into the community, rather than

51. Creator spirit, please let your
    soft lamp the soul of our poor
        land illumine and its am-
        ber comfort us. I am

        familiar with your grace when you
        call me to look out the window
            and quiet with its stars is heaven
            and men are doing what they can.

52. If I undertake to say
        the conscience of my country,
            I only do my duty.
            But, Lord, it was not I

        who chose it, but the hungry heart
        and level look that you allotted
            to me when you did burden
            with different gifts different men.

isolating and making them desperate. Certainly the old confession on the public square was a better idea.

It is doubtful that punishing some deters others. Varying the penalties has no statistical effect on occurrence, but only measures the degree of abstract social disapproval. And it is obvious that the great majority who do not steal, bribe, forge, etc., do not do so because of their life-style, more subtle influences than gross legal risks; other cultures, and some of our own subcultures, have other styles and other habits—for example, the youth counterculture has much increased shoplifting and forging of official documents.

The chief reason that so-called "moral legislation" has no influence in deterring vices is that temptation to the vices does not occur in the same psychological context as rational calculation of legal risks—unlike business fraud or risking a parking ticket. And it is likely that much authentic criminal behavior is compulsive in the same way.

There are inveterate lawbreakers and "psychopathic personalities" who cannot be trusted not to commit the same or worse crimes. (I think they will exist with any social institutions whatever.) It is unrealistic to expect other people not to panic because of them, and so we feel we have to confine them, instead of lynching them. But our present theory of "correction" in fact leads to 70 percent recidivism, usually for more serious felonies; to a state of war and terrorism between prisoners and guards; and to increasing prison riots. Why not say honestly, "We're locking you up simply because we're afraid of you. It is not necessarily a reflection on you and we're sorry for it. Therefore, in *your* terms, how can we make your confinement as painless and profitable to you as we can? We will give you as many creature satisfactions as you wish and we can afford, not lock you in cells, let you live in your own style, find and pursue your own work—so long as *we* are safe from you. A persisting, and perhaps insoluble, problem is how you will protect yourselves from one another."

53.   God bless my small home that
      I by habit decorate;
         avert the fire, fill the space
         if not by joy at least by use;

         make my daughter safe from the pest
         and my wife bear if that be best
         and many friends for many years
         learn to climb our steep stairs.

54.   I do not much collaborate
         not out of spite, but they are not
         my peers, I disregard
         their claims. It is too bad.

      But God He is my master and
      apprentice I wait His command.
         He asks me what I think of it
         and Him I tell my best thought.

It may be objected, of course, that many sober and hard-working citizens who aren't criminals are never given this much consideration by society. No, they aren't, and *that* is a pity.

23. Writing *Communitas,* my brother and I used only one methodical criterion: diminish intermediary services that are not directly productive or directly enjoyed, like commuting, packaging, sewer lines, blue books. These do not pay off as experience, but they clutter it up and rigidly predetermine it—you walk where the streets go. The social wealth and time of life that go into intermediaries cannot be used for something else. There are slums of engineering. Economists of the infrastructure do not think enough about this when they saddle underdeveloped regions with dead weight.

It is melancholy to consider the fate of John Dewey's instrumentalism, the idea that meaning and value are imbedded in means and operations, that the end-in-view is *in* practice. Instrumentalism was attacked as anti-intellectual, as base because it omitted ideals; but indeed it was an attempt to rescue intellect from being otiose and merely genteel. It was part of the same impulse as functionalism to rescue architecture, and industrial democracy and agrarian populism to rescue democracy. These meant to dignify the everyday and workaday from being servile means for Sunday goals. Now, however, we take it for granted that immense means are employed and operations carried on *instead* of meaning and value. No end-in-view, no experience, nothing practical. A university is administered to insure its smooth administration. The government makes work in order to diminish unemployment. A candidate runs for office in order to be elected. A war is fought to use new weapons. Only the last of these sounds harsh.

24. At best, survivals of the past, for example "Western culture," and the busy business of present society, must also be crushing weights on anybody's poor finite experience, unless he

55.   I talk to You because I have no one
      else, the two or three are gone
          to whom I told my murky thought
          because they cared for that.

      I said thanks to them, Lord, also
      more than I ever do to You:
          You are as close to my touch
          but I do not know Your love as much.

56.   I waited in the parlor, Lord,
          in panic for the messenger Your word
          for whom I had, as both we knew,
          no answer or excuse. But You,

      You, as often, Lord! had stolen
      through the back door into the kitchen
          and seated at the table quietly
          were pouring coffee for Yourself and me.

can somehow appropriate them as his own by education and vocation.

Most people in most ages pick up a good store of folkways and folk songs in the same way as they learn the language, however that is. They prudently manage to screen out most of the high thought and culture that is not for them, unless they are harrassed by schoolteachers; yet they also get wonder-full flashes of it: on solemn religious occasions; from works of high music, art, and architecture that have become like folkways; from important civic occasions that give food for profound thought, like constitutional crises, struggles for social justice, law suits; and most jobs and crafts, whether mechanics or farming or cooking or child-rearing, involve a good deal of fundamental science and high tradition that intelligent people pick up. Ordinary life can be culturally rich, and sometimes has been. It is a dubious society when the workdays, holidays, and election days do not provide enough spirit for most people, and we try to give a liberal education abstractly by lessons in school. It cannot be done.

In critical periods, alienated young people may choose on principle not to take on the traditions at all. At the end of the Middle Ages, the *moderni* declared they were throwing out the past and they deserted the Scholastic regent professors and set up their own colleges. The youth of *Stürm und Drang* threw out the courtly manners and morals. Today seems to be a similar time. Young people astoundingly may not know *Greensleeves* and *Annie Laurie*; they do not become thoughtful on days that commemorate events that happened thousands of years ago—like Huck Finn, they aren't interested in people who are dead; they take for granted what Harvey and Newton had to puzzle out; they don't care that Tyrannosaurus lorded it over the Cretaceous. The curriculum of a Free University might be, typically, Sensitivity Training, Psychedelic Experience, Multi-Media, Astrology, Castro's Cuba, History of Women, and Black Studies. These are not the major humanities, yet it is better to study what they *can* appropriate as experience than what they can't. (I am puzzled that they do

Four Little Prayers

57. My island by another week
has drifted like a rusty wreck
without a steersman. From the beach
with hopeless eyes I watch

her go. I would swim out
to her but You have also put
chains on my ankles. What,
Father, do You mean by that?

58. Yes, weariness and grief
is a fair description of my life
—I wonder if
others are better off.

I have also written,
like now, these facts down
and this has given me
pride if not much joy.

not study nothing, a deeply philosophical subject. They seem to have to go to school.)

Some of us, finally, live *in* the high culture, its spirit reviving in us and being more or less relevant to 1972, not with an easy adjustment. Our contemporaries are as likely to be Seami and Calderon as people we can talk to. People like us have a use. It would be woeful if the great moments of spirit did not survive. And the present institutions are lifeless if their spirit is not revived. But I don't know any method to teach what we know, namely that Beethoven, the Reformers, the authors of *The Federalist*, were real people and meant what they did. The great difficulty is that, in order to know them in our terms, it is first necessary to make the abnegation of learning them in their terms. And the less culture one has to begin with, the harder this is to do.

25. Vocation is taking on the business of the community so it is not a drag. If I find what I am good at and good for, that my community can use and will support, securely doing this, I can find myself further; and the social work is humanized because a real person is really doing it.

Having a vocation is always somewhat of a miracle, like falling in love and it works out. I can understand why Luther said that a man is justified by his vocation, for it is already a proof of God's favor. Naturally, it is psychologically easier if the family or community has provided intimate models to a child, and if it encourages him as he follows his own bent. It is harder if a child is poor or is restricted by his status, high or low, and has to take what offers or what he must. Faraday's career is a good example of both advantage and deprivation, and of the miracle. His father was a journeyman blacksmith. When he was adolescent, they apprenticed him to a bookbinder for seven years. Although he could hardly read, he used to take home the books of natural philosophy that came into the shop for rebinding, and copy out the diagrams. The clients talked to him—he must have been likeable as well as smart. They invited him to lectures. Because

59. How wistfully I envy
    without hostility
        the young who race and breathe
        without thinking of death.

    I used to try to know them
    and made advances to them
        who now seem like a different
        species in the environment.

60. In a panic and compelled
    as when once a devil held
        the knife to my heart and I
        had no choice but to obey.

    I was a child, I could not run away,
    my palms were cold and wet. Today
        but, Father of fugitives, I am old
        though my palms are wet and cold.

of his ability to fashion apparatus, at twenty he became the laboratory assistant of Humphrey Davy. So he had the right background, he had the right hardships to make him make an effort, and he had the genius of Faraday.

Our present practice is poor. Big Society has slots to fill; the young are tested for their aptitudes and schooled to fill the slots. There are no intimate models. The actual jobs are distant and unknown. Talent is co-opted; it does not develop at the youth's choice and time. A strong talent may well balk and deny his very talent. This is abstract.

But there may be an even more lifeless future, now widely proposed. The young must be trained to be adaptable to "play various roles." This will "free" people from being "tied down." Young people I have talked to like this idea; being "just human" means not limited to a vocation or profession. They want to be "into" various activities. As presumably Shakespeare was heavily into writing plays and Niels Bohr was into atomic physics. It is a curious view of personality and commitment.

26. To be a citizen is the common vocation. It is onerous unless one has an authentic talent for it, which I don't have, but we have to take over society as our (hopefully finite) experience or it takes us over infinitely. Even when I can only gripe, I write letters to the editor. I gave a collection of them the explanatory title *The Society I Live In Is Mine.*

A child or adolescent has the right to naïve patriotism, loyal pride in the place where he is thrown—he didn't choose to be born here. Without a sneaking nostalgia that there is *some* sense, honorable history, and good intentions in these people, we are in a harsh exile indeed.

For a child, even the idiot patriotism of nationalism is better than none. My little daughter, now nine, is going to an Hawaiian public school where they inundate the kids with "Columbia the Gem of the Ocean" and the Pledge of Allegiance, plus some pathetic Hawaiiana—the school is 95 percent quarter-Polynesian.

61.   His mother and I did our best, Lord,
        for Matt, and it was pretty good,
            and he for twenty years gave us
            the chance, without our disappointment
                or remorse.

      But now this leaves us nothing
      to blame or regret—only this bawling
          and the bright image that
          around the grave his friends confabulate.

62.   Our prudent Master has begun
        us at last to disburden
            of our long cares, Sally, too
            heavy often for me and you

      but we did not quit them. Oh
      as these things fall away we go
          lighter to our own graves, who are
          burdened also with each other.

63.   God of choice, in your real
        we two are wandering in hell.
            You know we chose to rear that boy
            rather than to live another way.

      When the corpse blocks the view
      what now are we supposed to do?
          Too much of us is now a failure
          for us to have a future.

But in New York she had been attending a "progressive" private school where instead of "America the Beautiful" they were likely to sing,

> O ugly for polluted skies,
> grain grown with pesticides . . .

and I am just as pleased that (for a few months) she is reading about the shot heard round the world and Thomas Jefferson without mention of his being a slaveholder. I see that it makes her happier to believe the noble rather than the base. It is touching.

27. "I have no idea what is the secret mission of the Navy vessels lying off my lanai in Waimanalo, but I wish they would get it over with and stop obstructing the horizon."—letter to the *Honolulu Star-Bulletin.* In fact they were practicing living in an underwater habitat built by the Oceanic Institute, nothing objectionable. But my resentment was that the Navy just sat there day after day, as if they owned the place.

I like Hegel's idea that property is an extension of personality; it is obviously so if we consider my tools, my clothes, my room, and my view of the horizon. And I would prefer to consider big capital property in the same light rather than that it is made purely by statute, state power. But it is largely our common inheritance that has been sequestered by a few. Property has come to mean not facilitating use, but excluding others from use.

Socialists object to any theory of natural property. They would in fact usually allow private use in clothes, tools, and so forth, but not as a natural right, rather as a right given by the collective. I think this is dispiriting; in order to assert my right and do my business, I would first have to take myself abstractly, as a member of all society. And of course prove my orthodoxy.

The issue of property has been wrongly put. The question is not whether personality extends into the environment—of course it does—but what kind of personality a man has. If he is exclusive and squeamish and rides roughshod over people, then

For My Birthday, 1967

64. O God who wear a heavy veil,
     I do not need to know what is real,
        yet lead me further where the real is
        although that way is rough. Your mysteries

     are probably too hard to live with,
     at least for me who draw my breath
        short by art and my perverse ideas.
        And now it has been six and fifty years.

65. God, You did exempt me from original sin
     and Your spirit with me often does commune,
        but You have plunged me into purgatory
        where faith and hope have little substance any
                more.

     I look in the mirror guiltless at my haggard face
     and I know that You hear my direct address,
        but I don't know how to pray or what to pray for
        and my eyesight is growing dim, Your creature.

66. Going mad with melancholy
     I write down words that make me cry
        —yet let me speak no ill of the
        Creator spirit who does not forsake me.

     We do not choose the real, she
     whispers and I obediently
        write it down, often in horror
        of the things that are.

his property will also be like that and will be objectionable. If he imagines that huge holdings do not enclose the commons, exploit the common wealth, and deprive other people, he is a fool. If the Navy would explain to me how it is temporarily appropriating that stretch of water for an interesting experiment, I might feel that *my* property in that stretch of water is being improved. I would willingly cooperate. My horizon would no longer be obstructed. —To be sure, I distrust *any* experiments of the Navy, but that it another story.

Nor is the issue between "private property" and "social property." Who would want to be private? We exist mainly, though not altogether, in community relations. To be a private individual is largely pathological. For a society to act as a collective is largely pathological.

28. The error of those who are mistakenly called "conservative" is not their laissez-faire economics. It is probable that competitive free enterprise is a more productive system than mercantilism, monopoly capitalism, or socialist collectivism. But as in the past, free enterprises still parcel out the commons as if it were on the market. They treat moral, cultural, and esthetic affairs that belong to the community as if they were economic affairs, e.g. giving access to the young, conserving the environment, helping the needy. But these are necessary for society to be tolerable at all. The tolerable background for any economic activity cannot be an object of economic activity.

And they make a corresponding mistake in their economics. In most of our present production, the chief value comes from the genius of Watt, Faraday, Rutherford, etc.; from the industry of our fathers who cleared the woods and laid out the roads; and from natural resources. We all happen to have inherited these gold mines. It is unreasonable for a few who control capital and thereby can make use of the inheritance, not to pay everybody royalties, e.g. at least the guaranteed income.

Te Deum for the Winter Solstice, 1967

67.   Thee God we praise for the short days
     of winter and the instant pause
       of the sun concealed this morning
       in the unbroken cloud. It is raining

     gently on the northeast and we
     have brought a dripping Christmas tree
       in, and put the golden star
       on top as every other year

     —the golden star and oh the blue
     that Matty used to pin below
       to represent Albireo
       the double in Cygnus. There are few

     things as beautiful in your creation,
     Lord, as this thing that my son
       sought out with his telescope
       and used to pin on our treetop.

29. Finally, in developed economies, both socialists and capitalists make a disastrous ethical mistake, mortgaging the present to the future. They put too much effort into profit, accumulating surpluses for new productivity and infrastructure, rather than first assuring a small profit for stability and livelihood. Growth Rate and Gross National Product become abstract fetishes, for which they sacrifice the present by skimping it, and take the life out of the future by overdetermining it.

Needless to say, the more the abstract Growth Rate flourishes, the more millions of people are likely to be left out and reduced to misery, for nobody pays attention to their petty concrete needs, which have nothing to do with Growth Rate and Gross National Product. There is a bigger pie to divide, but it can't be divided into inefficient items like food for a technologically displaced farmer or miner. In the long run he will surely be better off; in the fairly short run he will surely be quite dead.

Let me again quote the anecdote: "What," asked Coleridge, "about the little village that is rather self-sufficient and does not take part in the National Economy?" "Why, such a place is of no importance," said the Manchester economist. "Sir? are 500 Christian souls of no importance?"

In *Communitas* (Scheme III), we make the dumb-bunny suggestion of a dual economy with dual money: Let the big economy expand as madly as it wants, but see to it that there is also a small independent subsistence economy, producing subsistence goods at small-economy prices. (Recently, however, we have come to see that for ecological reasons the big economy can't expand like mad either.)

30. Equalitarians object to special privilege; for instance, they don't like it that my sheepskin promises to me "all the rights, privileges, and immunities" of a doctor of philosophy. But my ancestor Abelard and his students fought and suffered for those rights and immunities; we (maybe) need them to do our thing; I

Noah's Song

68. What is that lovely rainbow that abides
    upon the dripping moments till it fades?
    God promised me, though I am old,
    if I will work this new-washed field

    while my future vanishes past,
    something will come of it at last.
    This is the rainbow that abides
    on the dripping moments—till it fades.

am not at all willing to renounce them—indeed, I am a stickler for them.

Again, the issue is put wrongly. It is better if every person and his community of interest had far more rights, privileges, and immunities. Children have special rights, privileges, and immunities. Those who have worn themselves out bringing up children have special rights, privileges, and immunities—I guiltlessly say, "Young man, tote my bag." As a writer I need liberties and immunities that do not belong to a man who will never write a line; he does not care about freedom of the press, and in fact he won't defend it. The real issue is that many rights, privileges, and immunities that once had an historical warrant and enhanced experience and activity, have now become a racket. For example, professionals do need a peer group and to be professionally responsible only to their peer group, their oath, and the nature of things; but the economic blackmail of the medical associations is a racket. Lily whites may have a claim to club and eat with the like-minded, but not to deprive blacks of a share in the common wealth by segregating a restaurant on the main street, a neighborhood of a thousand houses, a national industry.

Professionals are bound to develop a ritual and secret language and mystify the laity, but this is acceptable (within limits)—their thing *is* a mystery and they have to do it their own way. What is unacceptable is for them to get the State to certify them as the only legal practitioners and exempt themselves from competition and criticism. The pretext is to protect the public from quacks; the effect is to increase the number of quacks, including those who are certified.

I am suspicious of equal law for everybody, like the *jus gentium* of the Romans that emerged with an Empire from which no one could escape. It is safer to have a bewildering tangle of unique prerogatives, and lots of borders to cross.

31. The main reason that Jefferson was a champion of freehold farming as a way of life was that it was independent of political

Four Little Prayers of Winter (1967)

69. I can't control, daily less,
        any of these circumstances,
            it doesn't happen as I forethought,
            I am trapped where I would not.

      But if I let be, as You counsel,
      look, it is unbearable,
            Matty is dead, Daisy ill,
            worse I don't will than when I will.

70. And it is not surprising, Lord,
        that the young I desperately wooed
            and me they paid no regard,
            now greedily around me crowd

      to pick at my exhausted love
      for wisdom that I do not have
            and still pay no regard to me
            though I am sick, plain to see.

pressures. It kept open the possibility of anarchy that he hankered for—"Let Shays' men go. If you discourage mutiny, what check is there on government?" If a farmer doesn't like the trend, he can withdraw from the market, eat his own crops, and prudently stay out of debt. If he has a freehold, they can't throw him off his land. (In Jefferson's day, he couldn't be drafted.) Other kinds of tenure have a similar privilege, academic tenure or seniority on the job, but of course the whole enterprise can shut down.

My own admiration for farming is its competence. The wonderfully direct connection between causes and effects, whether the seeds, the soil, the weather, the breeding, the plumbing in the barn, or the engine of the tractor; and of course growing it and then eating it. Needless to say, a farmer understands most of this only empirically, practically, not scientifically. He is not altogether in control. That too is very good; there are gods.

And Wordsworth had a good insight of the beauty and morality of rural life. The ecology of a country scene is so exquisitely complicated that we finally have to take it as just given. This simplifies it morally, we can relax a little. But I can't take the traffic or housing in Manhattan as given; it is an artifact and I have to do something about it. Also, the country scene has been so worked over for millions of years that it is bound to have unity and style, heroic in scale, minute in detail. But for various well-known reasons, the man-made scene is bound to be ugly. If people change their ways, it could become at least modest.

32. Sciences are sacred because they devote themselves—indeed, in a priestly way—to the natures not made by us, so they enable us to make sense and not live wishes, hopes, and nightmares. Being observant, humble, and austerely self-denying, dedicated scientists accumulate the reward of their Calvinist virtues. Great powers flow through them—which they can use to our disadvantage. Therefore they ought to bind themselves by oath to benefit and not harm the community, and it is better if this oath

71. What never was, what cannot be,
    what is no longer, are the three
        themes that men invent; and I
        live on by writing poetry

    talking to You who are
    deaf or do not choose to answer.
        Yet I prefer this conversation
        to that of men or women.

72. Doggedly I daily write
    the whispers of the holy spirit
        I hope I do not much distort
        by my misery distraught.

    Others have nothing but their sorrow
    —perhaps—how would I know?—
        but dry and brief is the phrase
        that I say, Lord, Thy praise.

is public and explicit, like the Hippocratic oath.

When, instead, they come on like petty clerks of the powers-that-be and as petty bankers of their own economic interests, the forces of nature are unleashed without human beings to interpret and exorcize them.

We others, artists and literary men, are easygoing toward nature and mix into our service a good deal of ourselves. So we accumulate little force, but it is domesticated. We do not need to bind ourselves with an oath, except not to censor.

33. Futurologists take current trends, that may or may not be good, and by extrapolating them for twenty years perform the sleight of hand of making them into norms that we must learn to conform to and prepare ourselves for. As a group they are extraordinarily slavish to the *status quo*—science fiction writers are often far more critical and daring. They seem to want to delete from primary experience its risky property of passing into the Next, beyond a horizon that very swiftly becomes dim and dark. Aristotle: "The past and present are necessary, the future is possible."

Luckily, human beings have enormous resources of anxiety, common sense, boredom, virtue, and perversity, to distort or reverse almost any trend you want.

The mania of planning for the future springs, of course, from the fact that current technology, urbanization, population, and communications are intractable—or at least the managers have lost their pragmatic inventiveness—so that it seems to be less desperate to grin and codify them. As Kafka advised, "Leopards break into the temple; make it part of the ritual."

My own prediction, however, is that there will be increasing disorder for twenty years, and that might be very well. Some things—some times—break up into fragments of just the right size and shape. People en masse learn only by being frightened anyway—ten thousand dead one morning of the smog, a city wiped out by an accidental bomb. It's not that we are stupid, but

(from *Homespun of Oatmeal Gray*)

Four Senseless Little Prayers of Convalescence

73. On all, the wicked and the innocent,
        blows the beautiful west wind
        and the warm sun sheds his light.
        But from them gather joy and benefit

        only those at ease in the Lord
        to whom all good turns to good,
        and hungrily we convalescents
        who face into the gentle elements.

74. Crazy for crazy, I believe
        that You will make the dead alive
        and from these evil things that seem
        I shall awake as in a dream

        —none hinders me, though I am in
        prison among men,
        to say the senseless sentence that
        saying makes me glad.

it takes a big fact, not a syllogism, to warrant a big response. If only the process of disorder is not aggravated by reactionary Law and Order, liberal Futurology, and radical Idealism.

34. I am bemused, as I spell out this politics of mine, at the consistent package of conservative biases, the ideology of a peasant or a small entrepreneur who carries his office and capital under his hat. Localism, ruralism, face-to-face organization, distrust of planning, clinging to property, natural rights, historical privileges and immunities, letters to the editor that view with alarm, carrying on the family craft, piecemeal reforms, make do, and let me alone.

No. It is not a possessive peasant nor a threatened small entrepreneur, but a small child who needs the security of routine. There is no father. Mother is away all day at work. He is self-reliant because he has to be. It is lonely, but nobody bugs him, and the sun is pouring through the window.

Where the emphasis in a philosophy of experience is on the foreground empirical facts, as in Dewey, we come out with a bias toward experiment and a politics of progressivism. Where the emphasis is on the phenomenlogy, the horizons and backgrounds of experience, we come out with conservation and conservatism. The difference is the old principle of acculturation from tribe to tribe: if the new item is a plough or a technique for baking pottery, it diffuses rapidly; if it is a change of tabu, child-rearing, or esthetics, it is resisted, it diffuses slowly or not at all.

Since as experience I want the concrete and finite, with structure and tendency, a Next so I can live on a little, and a dark surrounding, politically I want only that the children have bright eyes, the river be clean, food and sex be available, and nobody be pushed around. There must not be horrors that take me by the throat, so I can experience nothing; but it is indifferent to me what the Growth Rate is, or if some people are rich and others poor, so long as they are *pauvres*, decently poor, and not *misérables* (Péguy's distinction). I myself never found that much difference

75. Often have I dreaming frightened
    into puzzlement awakened,
        and most days have proved to be
        milder than my anxiety.

    On this analogy I'll say
    recklessly what pleases me,
        that one day I shall wake to my surprise
        and sweet confidence in paradise.

76. Since daily without hope I go
    daily forth my task to do
        —though wistful—and yet somehow
        despite despair I do go:

    this is the fact in which I write
    without belief the consoling thought
        that when I stand out of the way
        I shall stand in the sun happy.

between being very poor and modestly rich.

Idolatry makes me uneasy. I don't like my country to be a Great Power. I am squeamish about masses of people enthusiastically building a New Society.

The great conservative solutions are those that diminish tension by changing 2 percent of this and 4 percent of that. When they work, you don't notice them. Liberals like to solve a problem by adding on a new agency and throwing money at it, a ringing statement that the problem has been solved. Radicals like to go to the root, which is a terrible way of gardening, though it is sometimes sadly necessary in dentistry.

35.

Schultz, the neighbor's big black dog,
used to shit on our scraggly lawn,
but we feed him marrow bones
and he treats our lawn like his own home.

The kids of Fulton Houses in New York
smashed windows on our pretty block for spite;
we gave them hockey sticks to play with
and they smashed more windows.

The dog is an anarchist like me,
he has a careless dignity
—that is, we never think about it,
which comes to the same thing.

The kids are political like you,
they want to win their dignity. They won't.
But maybe their children will be friendly dogs
and wag their tails with my grandchildren.

A Prayer to Saint Harmony

77. In anguish I started from sleep:
   those I love I cannot keep
      from fire and polluted airs
      steep rocks and swirling waters.

   To mushroom and rabid animal
   my beloved are vulnerable
      and man and his machines may slay
      me or them I love today.

   The life is so precarious,
   Lord, that You parcelled out to us,
      many to a speedier death
      rush to have it over with,

   and I my dreams paint with fright
   in the horror of the night
      and cower in the dawn
      writing it all down.

   It means that I am raging
   within my soul sick and aging
      against my own and You the most.
      But blessed be the Holy Ghost

   in whom I know and say,
   and to Saint Harmony I pray
      who still makes my nightmares
      into music and calms my fears.

3. Beyond My Horizon—Words

36. It's a rudimentary experience I choose as mine, as if I were a simpler animal who doesn't have a long human memory, nameless yearning, creature anxiety, synoptic vision, and abstract language. How do I fill the gaps and make sense to myself? There are things that I do and say ritually, that go beyond experience. I can read them off as sentences, but they are empty of content. They are not perceptions, meanings, or feelings. They are theological, "the substance of things unseen."

I do not "believe" these theological sentences, that is much too intellectual a term. Not that I am skeptical by disposition; I am rather gullible. I entertain as likely almost any esoterica that people tell me with conviction, whether telepathy, orgone boxes, the Eucharist, or the relevations induced by psychedelic mushrooms. Having no wonders of my own, I marvel at other people's. Writing this, I have a sudden fellow feeling for Hume, who said he would walk a mile to hear Whitefield deliver one of his revival sermons. Except that we won't use these ideas as premises for anything that we might responsibly say or do.

I don't have a "faith," that is much too factual and erotic a term. I think of Karl Barth, one of the few modern writers whom I always read with empathy and pleasure, surfing on the wave of his thought, and his beautiful style speaks right to me. But he had a kind of substantial love affair with Jesus; and either Jesus made him happy or his faith did. My experi-

78. I am willing, God, to say
just how it is with me,
    the prayer best I can.
    But look, again and again

    to say that we are dying
    —this message is boring.
    "No, you do not need
    to write that down," He said.

79. I have no further grief in me.
    I can imagine, no, foresee
        the losses I will suffer yet,
        but my eyes do not get wet.

    When once the brass is burnished, Sire,
    there is no use of further fire,
        it is a mirror. But it can be melted,
        Sire, and destroyed.

ence contains no such fact or feeling and I am tolerably unhappy. Rather, I go along exactly with Kant in his little book on religion, "within the limits of mere reason." What I say here was already well said by him, that sticking to finite chunks of experience, it is inevitable to say words that go beyond their horizons and relate them to what surrounds them. But there is no sense to the spatial metaphors of "beyond" or "surround" any more than to other prepositional metaphors like "above" or "within," or to Kant's own nominative metaphors "things in themselves" and "symbols." Conversely, however, there is nothing in my finite experience that *prevents* me from saying such words! This gives me a crazy freedom of speech that I otherwise lack. Freer and crazier than if I were superstitious or had a faith. But of course nothing follows from this freedom empty and crazy.

The agnostic way of being of Hume and Kant is out of fashion these days, so people do not remember the positive exhilaration of it. (Today, nonbelievers are atheists.) Since the theological sentences of agnosticism are empty, it is possible to pick and choose and shape them, as the Deists, Unitarians, Universalists, and Ethical Culturists did, to be edifying. Or for poetry. Or just to live on a little.

37. Let me say again what I don't mean and do mean.

"Le coeur a des raisons que la raison me connait pas." This is crashingly true, but it is not what I mean. Pascal meant deep impulse, specifically his Christian impulse, as when Lawrence said, "Follow your deepest impulse." It was high romance for a mathematician like Pascal to make Pascal's wager.

"Credo quia absurdum." This is a powerful defiant idea, underlining the quite certain folly and Pharasaism of human judgments and moral values, and preferring to throw oneself on the Wholly Other. Writing about Ishmael and other outcasts in my twenties, I used to affirm the antinomian version of absurdity: let us rebel and sin in order to be touched by something divine, if only God's wrath.

80. My Bible text, when I grew
     old enough to be a Jew,
        was God to Abraham did say
        Lech lcha, "Go away!"

     I was thrilled, being a boy,
     at this portentous destiny,
        but to me You did not give
        a hundred fifty years to live.

     Hush. Where shall I go,
     Tour-Guide? Show, show
        me the map and circle
        the place with Your pencil.

81. This is a day the Lord hath made,
     rejoice in it and be glad.
        Our friends from foreign countries come
        because we have been true to them.

     The food we set upon the table
     is rich and good, as we are able.
        —Into the declining sun
        I softly walked away alone.

Angel:	Hypocrite! do you not live and breathe
	by the daily gifts here and here given you:
Ishmael:	So *You* say! when this mask of the world
	is stripped away, then shall we have full joy!

Nevertheless, though I am still not impressed by the wisdom or morality of righteous society, I am no longer tempted to deny what I think I do know, nor to act imprudently on principle.

But I like the safeguard of the Negative Theology of Jewish and Islamic philosophers—and from a different angle, of the Taoists. That whatever we say, is not true of God, nor is the contrary true. Simply, God is not a body and I know only about bodies, including myself. I mustn't take them as idols, including myself.

And yet—and yet—Why should I be fastidious of idols? What difference does it make? "Manlike my God I make." It makes no difference. But idolatry is stupid, and try as hard as I can, I cannot be stupider than I am.

38. Psychoanalytically, the obvious interpretation of inevitable but empty religious ideas is that they are obsessional rituals, like hand-washing or touching lampposts—their real meaning is repressed. I agree. Kant himself was the type of an anal character, with his scrupulosity, his routine, his sometimes amazingly harsh and strict sense of duty, his classifying, his aversion to instinctual feelings.

Yet it was Kant. Through middle age and a good old age, his work flowed on spontaneous, vigorous, brave, endlessly inventive and continually maturing, minutely attentive and boldly synoptic, and with a fine rhythm of style. We have to ask if Kant's way of being obsessional is not a good way to cope with the nature of things, in order to live on a little. I repeat it: the proof of a sage is that he survives, he knows how. "To work out your allotted span and not perish in mid-career: this is knowing." (Chuang-tze)

And there is something sweet in religious routines, once

Little Te Deum

82. I'm not in pain, I owe no debts,
     far as I know nobody hates
       enough to harm me, no disgrace
       tomorrow stares me in the face.

     Far as I know no new disaster
     is threatening my near and dear,
       and I am less by nameless fears
       beset than in my younger years.

     Thee God for this I therefore praise
     interim of undesperate days
       although it will not long endure.
       I do not live the various hour

     as the happy do or say:
     of homespun of oatmeal gray
       without a blazon is the flag
       that I hold up and do not wag.

drained of the virulence of belief. The cozy religiosity of the Danes, benignly ineffectual, is a good background for guiltless sex and common-sense pacifism. Every human child is necessarily brought up among tribal myths old or new. We must of course use our wits as best we can and strictly affirm and act our best judgment; but it is harsh and imperious toward oneself to try to root out one's archaic symbols. Especially since in the field of myths, new is almost invariably worse.

39. Finally, there is a wide divergence between the agnostic Enlightenment and what has proved to be the history of positive Science. But from the beginning they had different aims. It was the idea of humanism and the Enlightenment—of Erasmus and Montaigne, Hume and Kant—that the purpose of philosophy is to get rid of superstition so that life can go on; philosophy has no content. But the idea of positive Science—consider the program and utopia of Francis Bacon—was to accumulate a system of self-correcting natural philosophy by which we can live happily, with a useful scientific technology.

Naturally, during the sixteenth and seventeenth centuries, when humanism and heroic science were undermining the orthodox dogma, they were close allies. Indeed, before and during the French Revolution, they were for a time disastrously identified; together, they seemed to *be* the Englightenment. But the Rule of Reason enthroned at Notre Dame was bound to disappoint, if only because the scientists did not yet know enough.

Now two centuries later, however, when positive Science does know a wonderful and fearful amount, it has itself become the worldwide system of orthodox belief, heavily capitalized, recruited by a million trained minds—"there are more scientists alive today than since Adam and Eve." And it is hand in glove with the other powers that be.

It still disappoints, though its futurology promises infinite blessings. But to us threadbare men of letters, heirs of humanism and the Enlightenment, it is again the entrenched system served

Lines, and Little Prayer

Anybody could be shipwrecked,
who ventures, on a desert island
like me and waste away lonely.
I don't reproach me my bad luck
(I'm wretched enough as it is.)
I light fires. No one comes.
But anybody could be shipwrecked
like me on a desert island,
I don't reproach me my bad luck.
I light fires I light fires
I light fires. No one comes.

83.   Sometimes my sorrow is, God,
        so heavy my heart swells hard
            and I can go no further.
        Then let me sleep, Mother,

      and rave delirious
      in your embrace.
          Though you are anxious, you
          hold me stolidly the night through.

by a priestly caste, and it is again our duty to show how it is a superstition, so life can go on. (Oddly, the agnostic critique of Hume and Kant has become an intrinsic part of the orthodoxy, as conventional positivist logic.)

In his swan song, *The Conflict of the Faculties*, Kant spoke of philosophy as the "loyal opposition from the Left," whose duty was to harass the three positive Faculties of Law, Medicine, and Theology. I have no doubt that at present he would be criticizing the Faculties of Law, Medicine, and Scientific Technology.

40. For us who are thankful that we occupy only the ground that we cover with our two feet, the primary theological virtues are patience and fortitude, so said Kafka. (I think also of the comic portrait of Socrates firmly planted during the battle, not going out of his way to look for trouble, but every now and then giving a hard knock.) No doubt those who have a different kind of experience require different virtues.

Patience is drawing on underlying forces; it is powerfully positive, though to a natural view it looks like just sitting it out. How would I persist against positive eroding forces if I were not drawing on invisible forces? And patience has a positive tonic effect on others; because of the presence of the patient person, they revive and go on, as if he were the gyroscope of the ship providing a stable ground. But the patient person himself does not enjoy it.

In a passage that I often repeat, Goethe speaks of that patient finite thing the Earth. "The poor Earth!—I evermore repeat it— a little sun, a little rain, and it grows green again." It has a tonic effect on us. So the Earth repeats it, Goethe repeats it, and I repeat it.

Kafka himself, to be sure, was not persistent in his finitude. He was invaded by terrible paranoiac abstractions. (I take him as what he wrote.) Then his serene obsessional defenses broke down and he could not finish his stories.

The Guinea Pig, and a Little Prayer

I lightly woke to sweet and clear
chanting, the warbling of the guinea pig
loud in the dark, not like I used to hear him
squeaking across the floor, oh his voice
was really beautiful last night, he sang a tune.
I smiled as I dozed off.
              Now it is morning
and he is still and stiff—at 2 A.M.
dead in the playful jaws of the big dog.

Freddy, do not beat your dog in anger
and stick her nose in it, what does she know
of dying? Neither did I recognize
sighs of fright in the night,
sighs of mortal fright in the night, Freddy.

84. Who know my face wet with tears,
     Lord, where no one else is,
       and what I sing in the night
       is very earnest and sometimes sweet,

     but nobody seems to care for this
     though I am frightened, and my voice
       will afterwards be much admired
       by the English scholars, Lord.

41. Fortitude is to persist in one's task with an extra ounce of strength, after one has exhausted one's resources. As we say it in American, fortitude is to stay in there pitching. As I recall how often I have done it in bleak ball games and I have seen others do it, I realize it is a mystery.

But it must be a man's own ball game, exhausting his own natural powers, otherwise I will not get the extra ounce of strength, more than I have.—I learned from the most grievous event of my life, Matty's death five years ago, that it is useful to persist in doing what *is* one's own thing, exhausting one's natural powers very quickly when, in such a case, one has little grip on his own life. I wrote repetitive little poems about the one subject. And I was upbraided by an uncharitable lady for making literature out of the death of my only son. (My eyes are suddenly full of tears, but I will write down this *too*.) So I venture to give advice to other people in mourning: be sure that what you are doing is yours and persist in doing it; in everything else, willingly break down, suddenly bawl, run away if you feel like it.

Plato's Socrates defines courage as having an idea, and I suppose this helps one transcend his natural fear. But my hunch is that Socrates—it is in one of the early dialogues—said something less abstract: if one is *in* the situation, identifying with its meaning, he does not have a structure for running away; it does not occur to him, he is occupied. Then he will have an extra ounce of strength. He doesn't know from where; he has no leisure to ask.

42. I notice that I keep recurring to my authors of the concrete, the finite, the intrinsic: Socrates, Goethe, Kant, Kafka when he was well. It shows me again that I cannot learn anything different, and it shows that what I say is mine to say.

But I could spell it out as "developing" and it would come to the same thing. In my teens I was a Platonist and I wrote a long paper on the place of myths in the Dialectic Method: the plot was that it is the purpose of dialectic to bring us to a pause, paralyzed

85. No, neither with my eyes closed and You
    a presence warm that near I know,
      nor in the busy world and wide
      where I am Your friend open-eyed,

    but vaguely peering out to see
    a small room and I am drowsy
      and You seem to be everywhere
      in the room, if You are.

there might be evidence to clarify the meaning if I attend. By faith I am not caged in my finite experience; it has an horizon rather than bars; so I speak of it as "roomy enough." I am not alone, only lonely.

It is a latitudinarian notion of faith, like being sane. Nearly everybody behaves as if he had a world. A child runs headlong as though there will be gravity and ground, though he does not have nearly enough experience to believe this as certain as he acts it; it is built into his constitution. A speaker has a hearer in his language community, he does not think about it. Noah planted a vineyard because the Lord promised with his rainbow that something would come of it, there wouldn't be another flood. A scientist pursues his method as though the evidence was not planted to deceive him. I go to an orgasm by faith, I will not fall apart or not come down. We fall asleep by faith. I suppose there is nothing we do that we do not do by faith. "We live by faith."

I am paraphrasing Anselm's or Descartes' ontological argument: however we do proves faith. But there are no grounds for the faith. I cannot find anything in my experience that I would call faith. It is like Kierkegaard's Postman: one cannot tell, looking at him, that he is a Christian.

44. Perhaps the animal feeling of faith is trust, and perhaps at first, faith and trust are the same, like a child's trust in grown-ups or a dog's trust. These look animal. There is feeling on the face of the Adam of Michelangelo, trust already clouded with melancholy. But it is the genius of our families and institutions to destroy trust. Only God can destroy faith.

The Reformers seem to be right in saying that faith produces works but there is nothing that we can do to give faith. We can certainly do a good deal to remedy institutions that destroy trust.

"To them who have shall be given; from those who have not shall be taken away even that which they have." Yes. The muscular lad plays rough and gets still stronger. A lovable person is

(written since 1969)

Three Little Prayers on the Death of My Sister

87.   Lord, being sixty winters old
      I am not a child
         and ought not to need this or that person,
         but as an independent person

      do Your service in the city.
      But Lord, it is not so with me
         as I slowly turn and blink
         at where it is again forever blank

      and reach. New nothing is new bars.
      If I survive until the ground thaws
         in April, I shall put these ashes
         next to where my sister's nephew is.

loved and becomes still more open, radiant, and lovable. A person who is not anxious profits from psychoanalysis; an anxious person can afford to profit very little. And faith yields works. But the error of Geneva is to institutionalize this unfair distribution, coming on like God, deciding who is elect.

45. Theological hope is expecting the impossible. It is a terrible risk; as Goethe said, "By acting as though the impossible were possible, you soon make the possible impossible."

Certainly, for unlucky people like myself, natural hope—imagining, wishing, expecting—is an utter curse. It is disappointment. This has so often proved itself to me that I have almost come to understand how it works. I entertain a wild hope before I have laid a groundwork, or even *instead* of making a practical plan. My fantasy is an abstraction not in touch with the real situation, and it keeps me out of touch with it. In the order of my wishes, a random promise becomes a heated vision; in the order of other people's behavior, it has been quite forgotten. Most often when I am hopeful, nothing at all eventuates. If something does happen to eventuate, I am overwrought and act foolishly.

I do better, and suffer less, if I act with nonattachment, doing what is technically correct, expecting nothing; or acting generously, casting bread on the waters, expecting nothing. And if anything eventuates, if I cope with it like a present fact rather than the fulfillment of a wish.

Yet my extraordinary ineptitude contains a clue. A man could not possibly succeed so poorly unless he needed to fail. Either I am afraid to get what I wish for, so I see to it that I don't; that is, my excessive hope is a built-in prudence. Or I have despaired beforehand that my wish is what I want, and therefore I do not go about it practically to succeed. Yes, for the crazy glow of my hope, not its substance, is the color of what I really want, which is not possibly in the offing. And the horrible sinking of my disappointment is not for what I wished for, but because I am again reminded that I am not in paradise.

88.   Too many now are dead and alive
      for us to rise up from the grave
         at the last trumpet.
      We can no longer picture it,

         it is unmathematical.
      When the village was small
         and our ancestors a couple of dozen,
         we used to dream of our reunion.

89.   You teach quick and very hard
      in Your school, Lord.
         To me it is not always clear
         what the lessons are.

      I was unusually docile
      when I was in grade school,
         but I don't think I can pass
         in this upper class.

Theological hope is not delusory but blind. It is for a new heavens and new earth and I do not know the content of such a change. As I live from day to day, I do not feel any such hope, yet I live as if I had it.

—What do you want, my captain? what you want is impossible, therefore you must want nothing. "No. I am looking for the Northwest Passage to India. If I had made the world, that would exist."

46. Love is the experience that takes me beyond experience. Love has a concrete object and feeling, but it exists by promising to continue beyond Here Now and Next. As Rilke's Unicorn "exists by the possibility of being," love exists by the possibility of becoming. Thus it is the only theological virtue that is not empty of content, and from which something follows in my behavior. And I think this is why it has a privileged position in orthodox theology: it incarnates the god. He who will come.

To make a familiar distinction, sexual lust is experienced as Here Now and Next, it does not include an indefinite hope. But this difference, though real, is transient, for happy lust very soon turns into sexual love or into love without sex. Conversely, I doubt that one can have a good time lusting unless he is prepared to risk loving, losing himself. Orgastic pleasure is already a risk that needs both trust and faith. We love what has by-passed our blocks, so unfamiliar energy is released, that feels like risk.

Theologians make too much of the distinction between *agape*, self-giving self-losing love, and *eros*, love that tries to satisfy one-self and complete oneself. For also the latter is self-losing. And common language has always refused to make the distinction. Simply, the beloved fills the field of experience—"I am That"— and because I am diminished, new energy wells up, undomes-ticated, indefinite in meaning. It is crazy hope, except that now it seems to be practical, possible, having something to work at.

All love, whether sexual, parental, communal, or compassion-ate, is delusional. There will be no such ever-new world, if only because my anxiety reasserts me and protects me. (Saints, of

Four Little Prayers of a Sad Love

90. You notice, Lord, I am half pleased
     being sixty to be so confused
         and still not know how to cushion the pain
         of unlucky love. But it is again

     because the case is mathematical,
     God of games, like the Chinese puzzle
         that used to tease me when I was
         a child who could not do puzzles.

91. But woeful with the sin of waste
     which is the worst,
         Creator of the only world,
         I cut the knot with my sword,

     the nervous solution for a stupid
     problem that Alexander did,
         and still I don't know any better way
         just to live on another day.

course, can keep going.) But whether it is delusional or not, love is psychotic. It can be quietly psychotic, as I reasonably and prudently give myself away piece by piece.

Love creates new faith. Faith is given by grace, and love does the work of grace. It does so by actively making, or making up, a world for me in which I trust and where hope has substance; paradise, where there is no difference between grace and everyday practical action.

I notice, as I write this, how well it is all told by the Christian myth of Jesus incarnate as love and redemptive by giving himself, instituting a new heavens and new earth. But by my character I naturally prefer a literal analysis to the beautiful story.

> I say "I love you" more than I do, not lying,
> it's an hypothesis I hope will be surprisingly confirmed.

> But there is no rime or reason for you to love me too.
> Don't you say anything at all. Just be.

> I like to announce my intentions with a fanfare of six trumpets.
> I'm tickled when I sound like an old book.

The type of self-giving love is grown-ups' love of children. The unique gift that children give us is the opportunity to do for them, with no claim of return, therefore no resentment, therefore no guilt. It is depressing that this glaringly obvious fact is not told in the stories of God the Father, that *He* has a lot to be grateful for because of His creatures. Instead, He is represented as paternalistic; His guidance is very like a command, exacting obedience; His feeding seems to expect thanks.

On the other hand, those who, unlike the Creator of the animals, want to limit the number of children born, so that children may inherit an uncrowded Earth—they also tend to overlook that caring for the children is one of the few things that make life important from day to day, and there ought to be enough opportunity to go around. Friendship and neighbor-love are pretty

92. It was because of my need
     that I myself deluded
        that an unlikely thing could be
        and stubbornly pushed it, and I'm not sorry

     just sad. I gave of myself
     a lot and did not get enough,
        too bad for me. But him I did
        less harm than good.

93. Then O You dry fountain of actions and passions
     abundant beyond the equations
        of the conservation of energy,
        therefore smile again at me

     as distraught I go
     among the flowers of the meadow,
        the innumerable daisies
        and tangled vetch loud with bees.

complicated to manage. The ideal love of the artist or scientist is a daily fact for only a few. Love of society or mankind is abstract and begins to stink of idolatry. But everybody can love children.

Compassion, the virtue of the physician, is another spectacularly self-losing love. It is psychotic denial; the physician denies that the patient is really as he is. (Psychoanalytically, the compassionate man refuses to accept his own maiming.) And like other lovers, the physician sometimes transforms the world by making his denial stick. He puts it into question, which is crazy after all, finite experience or love? But in my observation, physicians are deeply angry people: "How dare you walk into my office in that condition?"

—A lifeguard, when he rescues someone, curses.

He has nothing to show for having lost himself. It was just remedial.

When Isaac was saved on Mt. Moriah, Abraham must have gone into a towering anger. The Bible, written as God's history, tells us nothing about this. All that heartache for nothing.

47. Beauty too proves something beyond experience, but it is not practical. The forms of paradise without the matter. As Kant put it, if the forms are adapted to our experience, we cannot experience the adaptation but only the pleasure of it. The forms seem purposeful for us, but they have no purpose. Plato speaks of beautiful forms as memories, of the jewels in the court of Jove.

Beauty mild is lively, but strong is terrible. When a strong beauty is just to see or hear but not desire, it makes me cry because paradise is lost—and there is nothing to do. If it is something to desire, then it is at peril that I resist what attracts me, however dangerous, unavailable, inappropriate, or perverse I may judge it to be. I must love it and suffer rather than be bored and caged as the horizon closes in. I cannot choose my paradise to be convenient, moral, or prudent. Pursuing the beautiful, I become still more inept.

94.   Maybe because of the rout we made
      or some fool tried to feed them bread,
         the phoebes left our porch where
         they laid their eggs year after year,

      and when I saw that empty nest
      very ashamed I saw the waste
         and raging of my days that drove
         away their sweet domestic love.

      But Merciful! they have flown
      no further than the attached barn
         through the wide door always open
         where now the two dart out and in

      with bugs for their gaping brood
      top of the birch post I made
         to firm the loft and left a ledge
         very apt to put a nest.

And then it is notorious that the beautiful appears only at the right esthetic distance and nearness. With art works, a good critic chooses the distance at which they show to best advantage. But with beautiful people, it is hard to attain the right distance, and impossible, I have found, to maintain it. One cannot eat beauty or fuck it. I have often lapsed into orgasm because the tension of beauty became intolerable for me. I have to sign it off.

The beautiful is not abstract; I cannot believe it is a delusion, and must respond with grief or desire; but it is only an esthetic surface, not practical for me.

It is like King Macbeth in the play: he is not an illusion of a king, he is a real king; but he is made of words, and one must not jump onto the stage and join in the battle. On the other hand, those contemporary plays in which I am supposed to join in, are not beautiful, and I get more excitement from action on the streets or with my friends. An artist can stage my beauty, but he cannot stage my paradise. A politician tries to stage my paradise, and it is the same purgatory.

48. I notice that I sometimes use the language of psychoanalysis and rarely a few terms of existential philosophy, but on the whole I prefer the language of orthodox theology to talk about the invisibles. Using words like faith, hope, love, paradise, purgatory, nonattachment, vocation, Way, Creation, koan, holy spirit, mana, Messiah, idol, Void, God, Karma, incarnation—mostly from the West, with a scattering from the East or from primitive religions.

These theological terms have been in use for thousands of years far and wide. We must assume that they have met a need, and they have certainly been polished by handling. Naturally they are resonant in a poet's vocabulary. They are very ambiguous and have been tormented by interpretation—though perhaps not more so than recent psychoanalytic and philosophical terms—but the contrasting interpretations are themselves ancient and have been spelled out in schisms and heresies. Hundreds of fine

Four Little Prayers After a Heart Attack

95.   An hour of panic while I fight
     for breath, and then all night
       in detail, rib by rib,
       exquisitely my muscles pick

     themselves apart, until at dawn
     I sink exhausted down.
       No doubt, Lord, though I do not see,
       that this is useful to me.

96.   A breeze of the evening
     and a thrush twittering
       in the sudden quiet.
       My pulse has begun to beat

     slower at last.
     A long freight train is rumbling past,
       I wanly wave and cheerfully
       the engineer toots at me.

brains have been busy about it, with millions of adherents, and much bloodshed to show that they meant something or other.

If I use this language when I talk to a person brought up in a Christian sect, we often quickly come to an earnest conversation about important matters of life or death. Using the other languages with no matter whom proves to be pedantic, cruder, and more polemical. To be sure, some Christians are puzzled and disappointed that, since we understand one another, I do not come out where they do. Richard McKeon, the Aristotelian, used to have this trouble with the neo-Thomists at the University of Chicago during the thirties; they charitably called him the Anti-Christ, because by making better sense of the texts he sometimes cooled off prospective converts.

Needless to say, the ones who are irritated if I say "holy spirit" or "Messiah" are the Unitarians and Ethical Culturists. Having (once) struggled to get rid of superstitious beliefs, they cannot tolerate even the language of theology.

But young people these days like this palaver, which seems meaningful to them, though their language is rather more eclectric than mine. There is a difference from my own youth when such talk was considered moronic and we had no language at all to describe our hopes or troubles. (I hit on psychoanalysis.) In the peculiar historical crisis they are now in, some of the young are so alienated that they finally germinate crazy ideas and will add to the history of theology, if there is any further history of anything.

49. Paradise is the world practicable. I do not mean happy, nor even practical so that I can make it work, but simply that I can work *at* it, without being frustrated beforehand. A task to wake up toward. If I work at something, I am happy enough while I am doing it—I don't think about whether or not I am happy. And if I have worked at it, if I have tried, I sleep well even if I have failed.

97. Since anyway I have been struck
    and I must stop all work,
        I am lucky not to be in New York
        but here where I can slowly walk

        from the orange lilies to the purple mallows
        and putter among the green tomatoes
            and crawl, with help, down the small hill
            to the river flowing at its own sweet will.

98. Tireless to excel,
        blameless because I did well,
            abandoned, I was competent
            in order to be independent

        —I had to be: all this taxed
        my heart that finally cracked.
            Now be my nurse and care for me
            while I whimper, or I will die.

This is a very modest criterion of paradise. To many people (how would I know?), there might be no reason to call such a world miraculous rather than the nature of things. For instance, John Dewey, who must have been a happy man, describes the nature of things as pragmatic through and through. But though I have faith that there is a world for me, I am foreign in it, I cannot communicate my needs, I do not share the customs, I am inept. So it is like a new world, I am as if resurrected, when the world is practicable. Therefore, until that moment, I put a premium on patience and fortitude.

The difficulties of the world, said Kafka, are mathematical. Given the spreading of space in all directions on a plane, it is infinitely more probable that our paths will diverge than converge. That you will be out when I phone and I will be out when you ring my bell—indeed, as Kafka points out, I was on my way over to your place. If several conditions are necessary for success, and each is moderately probable, the likelihood of their combination is wildly improbable. At every relay the message is distorted, and we did not speak the same dialect to begin with, but just enough of the same language so that we thought we were communicating. An unexpected stress, a lapse of attention, makes me vulnerable to other stresses, breakdowns, and accidents, so the rate of mishap is exponential. You get a flat tire and pull over, and step out over the edge and break a leg. These are the facts of life, no?

They are the facts of life for those who cannot abstract, who have only concrete and finite experience, like Kafka and me. We cannot take the vast numbers of possibilities as collective facts to manage, assigning them the infinite numbers Aleph, Beth, and Gimel. We cannot soar off the ground covered by our own two feet in order to survey the landscape. Since we have no values except in the tendency of what we are doing, we cannot make a plan of action to a far goal; we have no such goal, just the reality that we are dissatisfied.

A Prayer Sleepless

99.   I am sleepless every night.
      Is there—but I don't know what—
      I have not done and I must do
      so You will let me go?

      If I could sleep, Lord, maybe
      I'll dream of what I cannot see?
      —This offer is too sly,
      naturally You do not buy.

      Is there a horror
      waiting for me behind the door
      and therefore I dare not pass through?
      I don't know. I don't know.

      It is beautiful on this Hawaiian
      beach where my age is thrown
      and I watch with tired eyes
      the brilliant sun rise,

Then except by the miracle that events happen to converge in my poor Here Now and Next, my world is impracticable.

Fortunately, I have low standards of what is excellent as happiness.

In my politics—anarchist, decentralist, planning to leave out as much as possible, strongly conservative of simple goods that in fact exist—I have hit on a principle: Given the mathematical improbability of happiness, for God's sake don't add new obstacles.

In my morals, the cardinal sin is waste.

Consider the logistics of sexual satisfaction, a major part of happiness for most of us. Starting with the odd notion of sexual intercourse as a way of reproducing species, there is a rough carpenter's logic in dividing the human males and females equally, 50–50, to maximize the couplings; and then to attach a strong instinctual drive so that the animals will seek one another and persist in accomplishing the complicated operation of approaching, getting an erection, finding the hole, being receptive, and so forth. But a desire that is attached can become detached. The 50–50 possibilities are immediately drastically reduced by notions of beauty, inevitable childhood nostalgias and tabus, insecurities caused by factors that have nothing to do with sexuality, fetishism of other poles and holes. Since it is a complicated mechanism, Murphy's Law will certainly hold: if the parts can be put together wrong, they will be. And the machine has to operate in the frame of the rest of life and social life: being hungry and sleepy, sick, maimed, hampered by institutions and laws, poor and disadvantaged. Of course, since nature always operates with prodigal generosity and calculated waste, with a factor of safety in the thousands and millions, in spite of everything the human species is reproduced. The chances of personal happiness are trivial.

I have had half-a-dozen too brief love affairs (I am past 60), and in every case our virtue was to be practical, seizing chance opportunities, creating no obstacles, having no ideas in our minds, and

but it may be that the joys
of this world and new days
    are not for me—I know them too well
    (though I never had but a stingy sample)

and so I do not fall asleep
because I hanker after a longer sleep
    and this requires preparation,
    meditation, hesitation.

Come out! come out!
evil spirit
    who me possess.
    I cannot yet guess

who you are
but that you are
    whom by dim light
    I hunt in the night.

trying hard to make one another happy. Or put it this way: I offer myself all at once as a package, with the absurd conditions of my ineptitude, my fantasies, my perverse needs, and my crazy hope. I must be either frightening or ludicrous. But the one who became my lover was not put off and took me at face value. *Then* we were practical. And I say proudly, when we could not continue indefinitely as is the essence of love, the causes of our separation were not our doing, they were mathematical.

50. This world is purgatory. I have plenty of proof that I am not damned—I understand that it is heretical to say so—but I am being tried, I have no notion why. Maybe that's what I'm supposed to learn. Faith, having this-world-for-me, means that I am not tried beyond my capacity. The Lord will keep me alive, until He won't.

I spoke of myself as "unlucky," but it's not exact. Rather, my destiny has been to be continually hungry, balked, and deprived, but never starved, a total failure, with nothing. Continually in pain and handicapped by it, rarely incapacitated. Since I cannot believe that God is playing games with me, He must be testing me for my own good. Perhaps He is protecting me from the excesses of happiness, but gives me enough to keep me alive. If this is the case, He doesn't understand me well. For I do not become foolish, lazy, or arrogant, but sensible and grateful when I am happy, whereas this purgatorial regime keeps me inept and griping. Maybe I am wrong and if I were very happy I would be arrogant. I can't conceive what that would be like.

Sometimes I have the thought that God means to provide for me better but He can't. There are shortages. He doesn't have the technique to deal with difficult cases like me. He does well, considering.

Or I have the bitter, but not hostile, thought that God is an impatient artist. His conceptions are sublime beyond anything, like War Horse or the Big Dipper. Or they are deliciously odd, like wrapping up a bundle of levers, tubes, and wires—mechan-

100. Sometimes I said I was marooned
sometimes that I was imprisoned
or was in exile from my land
or I was born on the wrong planet.

But my daily fact, Lord,
is that awake I am a coward
and in my dreams that say the cause
I have lost the address, I'm confused.

101. Page after page I have lived Your world
in the narrative manner, Lord,
in my own voice I tell Your story.
Needless to say, I envy

people who dramatically
act the scenes of Your play.
Even so, the narrative manner
is my *misère et grandeur.*

It is our use
that some of us
insist on how
it is from our point of view.

ics, hydrostatics, and electronics—to be an animal. The execution is usually exquisitely minute. Yet there are clumsy or unfinished sentences, missing transitions, characters left hanging.

However it is, since I am in purgatory, I sing "Lead Kindly Light—one step enough for me." I often hum variations on the tune of it, half a dozen, a dozen, twenty, as I walk along.

51. There is a Creation, given to me. In which "everything is what it is and not another thing." (Bishop Butler)

I have tried to experience this givenness by dumb-bunny experiments. For instance, I am in the waiting-room, roughly aware of the rough structure of my chunk of experience. Can I notice the new that occurs that is not in that structure, and that will be given? A side door opens and a Puerto Rican woman in a green dress emerges. The effect is paranoiac; her appearance is portentous, a "delusion of reference," more tightly structured than all the rest. I dare not let the new be new.

The givenness of experience is what I do *not* attend to as I walk along, and there is always new space for it coming into being. Or when I pay attention to a meaning, and there is surprisingly more meaning, or less meaning, than I thought. Or I open my eyes, and I must take up from where I have been thrown. To Adam, I conjecture, the givenness of Creation was more apparent; everything happened to him for the first time. He lived in surprise. The givenness of Creation is surprise. But one cannot be surprised in the way one chooses to be surprised.

Kant, like Aristotle, held that existence is not a proper predicate that makes a scientific difference. There is no property of a real thing that may not be assigned to an imaginary thing and yet not make it real. Givenness is essential to any experience, but it cannot be experienced as such, nor scientifically measured. I must respect this opinion. Yet it is hard not to speculate that there is some extra energy in what is real rather than a possibility, a wish, or a dream. There are such heavy consequences from the reality of the real. Why could not this extra fire be measured, like

102. Save when my sight was narrowed
by sleepless pain, Lord,
    my experience has generally
    been roomy enough for me

and I haven't wanted to do
or learn anything very new.
    But now my life is daily narrowed
    to sleepless pain, Lord,

and I must learn to do
something very new
    just to live on. "Ah, but do you
    really want to?"

—that question, God, is wicked,
it is suicide
    which I have no choice
    but, Conserver, to dismiss.

Since to write I undertake
I will say my heart will break,
    censoring nothing; even so
    Creator Spirit, come thou new.

Oh, it is poorly between me
and my closest friend my body
    who will instantly betray
    our marriage stormy till today.

the heat that changes water into steam? Possibility is one "phase"; add the elixir and wish is another "phase"; and existing is another "phase."

I cannot think something into becoming real. But a reality can certainly make me think.

The present, says Whitehead, is holy ground. It is strange. It not only has the crashing weight of reality, but, unlike the immobile real past, it is frothing into indefinite possibilities. It is the Burning Bush of Moses that was not consumed, out of which God named Himself "Who Am."

It is the aim of Zen Buddhist exercises to know presentness as an experience, and it is said to be a mighty revelation. But of course the koan that brings infinite enlightenment is just the specious present: "What is the Buddha?" "Pass the salt." I have not been enlightened. (How would I know?)

In our Western tradition, however, both of the Jews and the Greeks, we have methodically won a mighty revelation of the Creation which we sum up by saying, There is a nature of things. *"Felix qui potuit rerum cognoscere causas."* By methodically studying the present appearances, we come to know, not the present, but the reality.

The Easterner seems to say that the present is God, the Westerner that it is the sacred text.

In *The Galley to Mytilene* I tried to distinguish the Actuality that weighs down the ship carrying the message of doom; the Reality of the confusion of the sailors in which the ship is foundering; and the Existing Moment on whose wings the new ship is bringing the message of clemency. But it is the same ship. I wrote, "Try! and I shall never be able to distinguish them."

History, what has happened and happens, has a privileged position over possibilities, noble ideas, lost causes. It is Creation, and thenceforth the given. And I can understand why Vico, Hegel, and the others have taken it to be God or His demiurge. But I think that these philosophers too much mean by history the

103. What is the Buddha? "Drat!
pass the salt," the sage spat.
I understand. I understand
but I am not enlightened.

Am I enlightened? How would I know?

104. If from the bottom of sleep would summon
me forth mysterious some dream,
or if these golden suns that break
on the purple water would say "Awake

and choose to live."—Neither has happened.
But my wife and neighbors tend
me kindly and from far away
they phone good wishes night and day.

Maybe it is enough to heal my wound
just because the world turns around.
I never did understand my meaning.
I rarely have looked forward to the morning.

history of institutions, nations, great men, Society. If God is history, it includes the history of me.

52. The Creator Spirit visits me and treats me as a familiar, but I have not experienced this. I have never felt inspired. (I think of Cupid and Psyche.)

After a work is finished, I can usually show in fine detail how it is made, how the parts hang together, and why it works; and I can often offer shrewd guesses as to why I made it, what it has done for me, and what it is for. But none of this is experienced by me while the work is in progress. And indeed, the words and their relations, and the choices to be made, are so indefinitely numerous that it is mathematically impossible that I could manage them, except to keep at it and to steer.

The coming of spirit is new creation. From nothing. In fields where I have any firsthand acquaintance, literature, social institutions, therapy, the relation of master and apprentice, the conservation of energy is not *prima facie;* it is farfetched. Nobody in such fields would think of it. The weight of evidence is overwhelming that there are continual flashes of creation, order made from nothing, against entropy. There are initiative, invention, and insight, and there are routine, falling apart, and entropy, but the entropy does not look like the dominant trend. We would not see the passage of the prophetic into the bureaucratic if we were not struck by the prophetic. Sudden and interesting. My bias is to deny the theory of conservation.

The question is if the physicists who affirm conservation are not using it as an a priori principle, proving it beforehand by their language of equations and by their attitude toward the matter they work on, which is always *natura naturata,* never *natura naturans.* If they included themselves presently experimenting in their operational account of the experimental situation—as indeed the operational language requires—maybe they would come out differently. I don't know.

I think that a physics without the conservation of energy would

105.   How blue it is! between the water
and the sky stretches taut
    the silken thread of the horizon
    and the sun's corona

wraps me around. Maybe my heart
won't crack a little while yet
    and I can take a swim on this
    practical hypothesis.

106.   When I think of the subtile balances
of chances and circumstances
    that kill or make men thrive,
    O Lord of Moments give

me onward a few happy years
as You can—if my desires
    are modest and they do not much
    the great Frame of the Likely wrench.

look like Taoist magic. It might even be technologically productive. They say that the Master rode the whirlwind, the only one motionless in the storm.

53. I do not know of any sacraments that take me beyond experience. Love takes us beyond experience, but we love by grace, and I am puzzled at those who urge me to love my neighbor (though I think I ethically understand what it means to be a sociable, considerate, and cooperative neighbor).

Yet there are two religious exercises that confront the invisibles: confusion and prayer. It is odd to call confusion an exercise.

Experience is torn by confusion, and the darkness seeps through. "All have smiles on their faces, as if going up to the Spring Festival," says Lao-tse, "only I am murky and confused." Murky, with the solemn face of an animal, not much in its mind. But confused because, unlike the animal, the sage has little grip on life, so his experience doesn't make sense, it has no tendency. He is standing out of the way.

The sage is at a loss on ordinary occasions; he does not need "borderline situations" in order to go blank.

Buddhists and Western contemplatives attain clarity by their nonattachment. Therefore I say they are abstract; by concentration they have willed themselves out of the stream. The Taoist sage is scattered—drowning—as he relaxes his grip on life. His insight becomes still dimmer than it was, and he is face to face with the void. Which may or may not yield up a treasure.

For those of us who are used to making sense, however, it takes a big deal to be baffled. Typically, we have tragic dilemmas, the clashing of absolute duties. To carry these through is very much a Western plot. In the *Gita*, when Arjuna is in a tragic dilemma, the Lord advises him to act with nonattachment, and evil will not cling to him any more than water to the lotus leaf. But the recipe of our Greek tragic plots is decently to affirm both contradictions, to sink into them deeper, till the protagonist becomes exhausted and then confused and then goes blank, all with a good con-

107. Both ways, real world, I defy
you because it is necessary:
    first I will what cannot be,
    now what might be I will destroy!

    —so saying I fell dizzy down
upon the ground that reeled around
    and the young man led
    me home unsteady to my bed.

108. I shall not die, for I shall live
and say His works. He did not give
    me unto death, though me He hurt.
    Open up to me the gate.

109. I ask the Lord, "Who are You?"
though I know His name is "Spoken to."
    Hoping but I am not sure
    His name might be "I am who answer."

    With certain faith let me continue
my dialogue with Spoken-To.
    Hope has always been my curse,
    it never yet came to pass.

    The crazy man that you meet
talking to himself on the street
    is I, please gently lead him home.
    Creator Spirit come.

science. As Kant says, it is one of the functions of God—not my business—to see to it that, if I do my duty, I can nevertheless be happy. "You do not need to finish the task," said Rabbi Tarfon more gently, "neither are you free to leave it off."

When we are baffled on a grand political, national scale, we hope for the coming of Messiah. For instance, the probability is high (95 percent) that atom bombs will destroy my friends and children. Our statesmen are not going to solve this (100 percent). Yet we persist in our institutions because of the coming of Messiah.

Statistically, as I grow old, I inevitably see more and more the death of my colleagues and dear ones, and I am confused. I understand that all flesh is as the grass, and very good. I see, too, the ever unique woe the survivors suffer—what we knew as moving and responding and initiating movement, is a worthless corpse, and it is too late for many things; yet I understand, I *understand* that we must try to mourn it through. I understand these two ideas but I cannot grasp them in one vision. It is too sublime for my finite experience and I become confused.

54. Prayer is the opposite exercise. I gather together my finite experience that is scattering in confusion. Here it all is, like an offering. Thus I disown my experience and again come face to face with nothing.

I do not pray for anything; whom would I ask? When I am not needy but happy, there is also no one to thank. But I pray by saying just how it is with me, and that is my prayer.

If we pay close attention to an isolated word, instead of scanning it in use in an ongoing sentence, it becomes odd and crazy. It is the same with any object that we gaze at intently, unless it is something beautiful and loved that keeps meeting us with new meanings. (But even such a thing soon becomes exhausted and looks monstrous.) So, by publishing my chunk of experience as literally as I can, I get rid of it.

Lines and Little Prayer

If I told you, child,
I heard Johanna Gadski
singing Brunhilde;
naturally I couldn't judge
if she was any good
as well as old and cracked,
but it was the first I ever heard
the Rhine Journey and I was astounded,
in the top balcony, way on the side.
The intervening half a century?
was empty, nothing happened.
What *were* the heat and passion
I worked up in my politics
and in my jealous fits?

110.   The day is cloudy but toward evening
the sky is clearing
    and the sunset is vivid.
    Swiftly what is hid

behind the colors the one dark night
will show herself to brave men, but as yet
    not to me who dare not
    seek her and go out.

Unfortunately, I have then thrown it to you, like the Orthodox confession in the village square.

When I do what is called "thinking," muttering to myself, I never use words like God or Faith, and they are in no way premises for my behavior. When I talk to other people, I sometimes use them, but not authentically; I might use such language, as I have said, to facilitate earnest conversation with a believer, though I am not a believer; or I might use it to cut short a boring conversation with an unbeliever, when I am too tired to explain myself better. When I write, however, I readily use this vocabulary and apparently seriously. How is this?

In *Defence of Poetry*, I suggest a possible reason: "Maybe it is that when I think or talk to myself, I am embarrassed; but when I write, I am not embarrassed"—since writing is my free act. But there could be a simpler reason, more *prima facie*, more what it feels like; I use this language because it is a poetic convention, a traditional jargon, like wearing old clothes because they are comfortable. It means nothing. A free act is an empty act, except as an act. It means what is the genius of the language of billions of human speakers—not my business. As a writer my business is only to be as clear as possible and say a work that has a beginning, middle, and end.

ABOUT THE AUTHOR

PAUL GOODMAN is the author of twenty-four books, among them *Growing Up Absurd* and *Making Do.*

ABOUT THE EDITOR

RUTH NANDA ANSHEN, philosopher and editor, is the author of *The Reality of the Devil: Evil in Man*; and plans and edits PERSPECTIVES IN HUMANISM, RELIGIOUS PERSPECTIVES, WORLD PERSPECTIVES, CREDO PERSPECTIVES, and THE SCIENCE OF CULTURE SERIES.

72 73 74 75 10 9 8 7 6 5 4 3 2 1